WARNING: the document you are about to peruse
is full of Racist Propaganda!

South Africa: A Visual History

South Africa: A Visual History

1972

Visual Publications

P.O. Box 845, Johannesburg

Typography and production by Artem Creare
Cover: Marc Achleitner
Set in 10 on 11 pt. Univers Medium/IBM
Set, printed and bound by
Perskor, Doornfontein, Johannesburg (10867)

1972 Edition — Published 1973

ISBN 0 628 00427 3

ERRATA

SOUTH AFRICA: A VISUAL HISTORY 1972

Page 7

1st Column — heading of graph should read:
Gross Domestic Product

The Republic of South Africa, situated at the southern tip of Africa, is not only famous for its vast deposits of gold, diamonds and other precious minerals but for the problems posed by its multi-racial and multi-national population structure over the past two decades. With a total area of 1 222 543 square kilometres (471 982 square miles), larger than West Germany, France, Italy, Holland and Belgium combined and it is home for more than 22 million people consisting of several black nations, a white nation, a mixed race group and nearly 700 000 Asians. Ten major languages are spoken in South Africa. The country has been self-governing since May 31, 1910 and completely sovereign since 1931. Pretoria is the official seat of government but laws are made in Cape Town where Parliament meets. Contrary to popular belief, South Africa is not primarily an agricultural or mining country but an industrialised state, the only one in Africa. Johannesburg, with a population of 1,5 million, is the largest city; Cape Town, founded in 1652, is the oldest. The country is served by a network of roads totalling 320 000 kilometres, 31 000 kilometres of rail track, as well as scheduled air services. About 500 newspapers, periodicals and journals are published, including 22 daily newspapers. There are 16 universities and 15 000 schools. The country attracts about 40 000 immigrants every year from Britain and Europe. South Africa has also been administering the territory of South West Africa since 1920 as an integral part of the Republic, as provided for by the erstwhile mandate of the now defunct League of Nations. South West Africa, as big as France and West Germany combined, has a population of only 700 000.

Introduction

This series provides a year-by-year written and visual record of South Africa's evolving history to those with an interest in the country's contemporary development.

An invitation to page through this annual is, therefore, an opportunity to embark on a journey into the past that is not as dead or irrelevant as we are sometimes inclined to think. You can make many such journeys, for each year outlines the itinerary, scenario and personalia of a completely new one, which you can undertake whenever you wish.

To those on foreign shores who may read about events in South Africa in the press, or view some facet of its complexities on television; to those abroad who may have a personal interest in present-day South Africa — who have friends and relations living in this country; to businessmen, scholars, tourists, friends or foes, a *Visual History of South Africa* will provide a useful service. It is a window on a large and tremendously important part of Africa which will inevitably become the focus of international interest in future. South Africa is the technological and industrial giant of the African continent, its major military political power, commanding the life-line of the Western World, the strategic Cape of Good Hope sea-route. More than 50 of South Africa's vast treasure-house of minerals are mined — including almost every mineral needed to sustain a modern industrial economy. The importance of these minerals to the industrial states of Western Europe, America and Japan, is assuming greater and greater proportions.

An illustrated, living, and chronologically continuous record of outstanding events in South Africa is a virtual necessity, too, for schools and universities, since no part of South African history is as neglected as its contemporary history.

The student at school or university is, however, not the only one with a direct interest in the history of his times. If someone were suddenly to ask *you* to recall the really outstanding events in South Africa during the previous calendar year, in, for instance, sport or politics, would *you* remember? How would you fare when asked about events of two years ago? Or five? or a decade? These events may, directly or indirectly, have affected your career, your income, you political views. One fact will soon emerge: the incredible rapidity at which one forgets events of even profound national importance. Perhaps you have personally witnessed some of these occurrences. If not, you will have heard or read about them. They may even have involved persons or places known to you.

Faced with these questions, then, to which factual sources can you turn? Memory is embarrassingly fallible. And which of us has the time or inclination to consult back-numbers of newspapers and magazines simply to satisfy a passing flash of interest in contemporary South African affairs? Formal and official year-books? Once again, how many of us would go to the trouble of struggling through voluminous tomes filled with specialist facts and figures?

Visual History of South Africa, however, provides you with your own easy-to-check record at home. There is a summary of events and descriptive captions to each of the photographs selected. They provide visual pleasure for young and old, not just once, but time and again — as often as the opportunity to pause and delve arises. These volumes are equally at home on the library shelf, on the coffee table, in the livingroom, in the waiting-room, or on the office desk.

That most elusive of beings, the so-called Average Citizen, is sometimes motivated to take a quick backward glance at the highlights of yesteryear. Often he wants to re-align and re-adjust his perspective on the passage of events over time — or simply to satisfy his curiosity. A short visual resumé of the nation's contemporary scene is what he needs — but this can also provide a rewarding educational exercise — a manifestation of a civilized way of life. If our Average Citizen seeks a source that will concisely and meaningfully present the annual highlights of his country's development, he is probably looking for a suitable *visual* record. Such a record must be aesthetically and intellectually satisfying; a sequence describing real-life situations in a colourful and factual manner.

Visual History of South Africa provides such a record. It does more than that: it instils into the viewer the realisation that history is being made every day; that we are the audience and sometimes even the actors in a real-life drama; and that learning more about South Africa links us, in history, to the many communities of which our country is comprised.

THE EDITORS

SEPTEMBER 1973

1972 In retrospect

POLITICS AND GOVERNMENT

The constitutional and political progress of the Republic's Black Homelands towards independence escalated sharply in 1972 when no less than three Homelands, Bophuthatswana, the Ciskei and Lebowa, formally attained the status of self-governing territories within the Republic of South Africa.

In establishing the new self-governing territories, the South African Government reaffirmed "its irrevocable intention to lead each separate national group step by step and in an orderly manner, to self-government and independence".

Self-government entitled the new territories to an own Cabinet, Legislative Assembly, official language, flag and national anthem. Together with the Transkei (1963), the development meant that the Homelands of four of the Republic's eight Black nations had attained self-governing status. Indications were that more Homelands would be declared self-governing territories in 1973.

At the beginning of the year the South African Government announced that it intended stepping-up considerably on planning for the greatest possible geographical consolidation of the historical Black Homelands. It was anticipated that major consolidation plans would be completed before the end of 1973. But by October, the consolidation programme had proceeded so well, it was stated that there was every hope of submitting completed plans for all the Homelands to the central South African Parliament in 1973.

The year also saw extensive changes in the central South African Cabinet. Five new Ministers and four new Deputy Ministers were appointed, while a redistribution of portfolios also took place. In September, an overwhelming vote carried the Minister of the Interior, Dr C. P. Mulder, to the leadership of the National Party in the Transvaal Province, the country's most powerful political province. This followed the surprise announcement by the veteran Minister of Transport and Leader of the House of Assembly, Mr B. J. Schoeman, that he was relinquishing the Transvaal leadership and intended retiring from politics in a few years' time. This development was seen as an indication that Dr Mulder had become heir apparent to the premiership.

The Republic made further progress in strengthening its all-round defence capabilities. The first ultra-modern submarine base in Africa was opened at Simonstown, co-inciding with the arrival of the Republic's third French-built submarine. Another example was the completion of phase two of the Republic's extensive national air defence radar system — this included a highly sophisticated underground command complex, one of the most modern in the world.

EDUCATION, SCIENCE AND ENVIRONMENT

By dint of solid achievement and sustained progress in the spheres of education and science, South Africa once again underscored its leading position on the Continent. The Council for Scientific and Industrial Research (CSIR) in particular continued to play a major role in various fields of scientific endeavour. A Council team of medical electronics researchers, e.g., developed a tiny radio telemetry system for maintaining the electrocardiogram of cardiac patients. In November, the Council's experimental autogyro (developed over eight years) had its first successful flight — the first autogyro of its kind in the world to reach the operational stage. The CSIR also organized and participated in a large number of symposia covering a wide spectrum of educational and scientific research.

A Chicago research team headed by South African-born Dr Francois Booyse, was awarded the 1971 Jane Nugent Cochems Prize for the most outstanding contribution in the field of basic vascular problems. In April a Black mother, Mrs Grace Nkoane, became the first woman with two artificial heart valves to have borne a child, further proof of the Republic's leading role in the field of cardio-vascular medicine. The first South African Nursing Association Congress to be held in a Black Homeland gathered at Umtata in the Transkei in July. The following month the first Cancer Congress to be organized in South Africa took place in Johannesburg. In the same month South Africa's first total liver transplant operation was performed.

Various parts of the Republic were photographed for the first time by the 'Earth Resources Technology Satellite' (ERTS) launched in June by NASA. Professor E. M. van Zinderen Bakker, of the University of the Orange Free State, and Mr P. A. le Roux, attached to the Weather Bureau, were the first recipients of the South African Antarctic Association's Gold Medal, an award made for work in the sub-Antarctic islands. An academic milestone was achieved when the first Black South African received his doctorate in physics from the University of South Africa. Another happy academic event was the University of the Witwatersrand (Wits) celebrating its 50th birthday. Wits also saw a dream come true when its nuclear research unit inaugurated its new Tandem Van de Graaff Nuclear Accelerator, one of the largest in the Southern Hemisphere.

Scientists of the National Fuel Research Institute in Pretoria made headlines with the world's first fully smokeless stove designed as a do-it-yourself construction set. The Institute also designed a Diesel engine converted to run virtually smokelessly on dieselene. A further blow for the battle against smoke pollution was struck by the Iron and Steel Corporation (Iscor) with the announcement that it planned to increase its spending on antipollution measures over the next ten years from R100 million to R120 million, amounting to nearly ten per cent of the Corporation's planned capital expenditure on works and mines. The South African Government also stepped up its campaign against environmental despoliation, announcing, e.g., the speedy introduction of strict anti-pollution measures, particularly the kind of environmental hazard caused by oil spillage in South Africa's coastal waters. Further good news for environmentalists and ecologists (both amateur and professional) emanated from a conference on international parks in the U.S.A., where it was widely conceded that the Republic was tops in game ranching research and probably also in nature conservation in general.

ARTS AND ENTERTAINMENT

Judged by the activities of the Performing Arts Councils of the four provinces (Pact, Capac, Napac and Pacofs) and the number of internationally celebrated artists and entertainers who visited South Africa during 1972, the arts and entertainment experienced a vintage year. These top-class artists and entertainers, whose work and performances ranged over practically the whole gamut of serious art and light entertainment, once more underscore the pleasing fact that South Africa is rapidly becoming one of the most popular and rewarding 'hunting grounds' for many of the world's top performers in the arts and entertainment. Many of these guest artists and entertainers visited the Republic at the invitation of the four provincial Performing Arts Councils, notably those of the Transvaal and Cape. Capac scored a notable triumph with Pieter Toerien's production of 'Dial M for Murder', starring the Oscar-winning film star Joan Fontaine. Other popular Capac presentations were Mozart's *Don Giovanni* and Puccini's *Madame Butterfly* and three Spanish ballets (with Phyllis Spira as principal dancer).

PACT enhanced its reputation as a major bastion of the arts with major presentations such as Verdi's Rigoletto (with Luciano Saldari from Italy in the role of the Duke of Mantua); the ballet *Giselle* (with Russian ballerina Natalia Makarova and Ivan Nagy the principal dancers); the ballet 'Cinderella' (with Sir Robert Helpman, Sir Frederick Ashton) and several outstanding plays e.g. Genet's 'The Maids', 'Alice's adventures underground' (adapted from Lewis Carroll's famous work), Karl Wittinger's '*Do you know the milky way*?', Schiller's '*Maria Stuart*' and Tsjechow's '*Seemeeu*' (Seagull).

In Natal, NAPAC stepped into the limelight with Guy Bolton's '*A Man and His Wife*' and two excellent productions for children, '*Winnie-the-Pooh*' and '*Puss in Boots*'. Natal audiences also delighted in successful presentations of *Carmen* and *Cavalleria Rusticana*.

In the Free State PACOFS' Afrikaans production of Dürrenmatt's '*Die Ehe des Herrn Mississippi*' attracted enthusiastic audiences.

Famous names figured among the many artists, entertainers and ensembles to visit the Republic during the year, such as Victor Borge (Danish musician); Piérre Fournier (French 'cellist); American film stars Yvette Mimieux, Jerry Lewis and Robert Mitchum; Teresa Berganza (Spanish coloratura mezzosoprano); Georges Themeli, the blind Greek pianist; Horst Jankowski (German jazz pianist); Rolf Kuhn (German ace clarinetist); Aleka Katseli (Greek actress); Kenichi Nishida (Japanese painter); conductors Hugo Rignold (Britain), Louis Fremaux (Britain) and Henry Arends (Holland); Joan Fontaine (famous British film and stage personality); the Melos Quartet (Germany's top string quartet); the Opitz Formation (the celebrated German dancing team); the renowned violinists, Robert Gerle (Hungary), Robert Soetens (Belgium) and Salvatore Accardo (Italy); prima ballerina Margot Fonteyn; and the vivacious American stage personality and singer Eartha Kitt.

South Africans were justifiably proud of the S.A.B.C. Youth Orchestra's accomplished performance at the 1972 Festival of Youth Orchestras in Lausanne and with the continued successes of soprano Joyce Barker (in Britain) and Joseph Gabriels (in West Germany).

INTERNATIONAL AFFAIRS

The visit of the United Nations Secretary General, Dr Kurt Waldheim of Austria and of his personal envoy, Dr Alfred Escher of Switzerland to the Republic of South Africa for talks with the government on independence for the people of the territory of South West Africa (referred to as "Namibia" by the U.N.), dominated the news. The Republic has been administrating South West Africa as an integral part of South African territory the past 53 years. Inviting the U.N. Secretary General to visit South Africa the Prime Minister, Mr B. J. Vorster, said that Dr Waldheim would be received with the same courtesy and hospitality extended to Dag Hammarskjöld during the late Secretary General's visit to South Africa. Mr Vorster made it clear during the traditional no-confidence debate in Parliament in Cape Town that South Africa did not recognise the jurisdiction and control over South West Africa claimed by the U.N. General

Assembly but, since it was South Africa's oft declared objective to lead the peoples of South West Africa to self-determination and independence, the government was quite willing to discuss this matter with the Secretary General.

Dr Waldheim arrived in South Africa on March 6 and after preliminary talks with the Prime Minister in Pretoria left for an inspection of South West Africa. He subsequently told a press conference he believed that both South Africa and the U.N. desired self-determination and independence for the people of South West Africa. Before returning to New York on March 11, Dr Waldheim was guest of honour of the Prime Minister at a state banquet in Cape Town at which he said he regarded his visit as a "breakthrough". He thanked the Prime Minister for enabling him to visit South West Africa and also for making it possible to meet a cross section of the people of South West Africa.

Early in May the Foreign Minister, Dr Hilgard Muller announced that he was going to New York to continue discussions with Dr Waldheim. Further talks also took place between Dr Waldheim and South Africa's Ambassador to the U.N., Dr Carl von Hirschberg.

Following speculation in the press that a United Nations presence was to be established in South West Africa the South African Prime Minister, Mr Vorster, reiterated in Tsumeb (mid-June) that his government did not recognise United Nations claims to control over South West Africa. Mr Vorster said that the basic difference between South Africa and the U.N. was that the latter believed in self-determination for the territory as a whole whereas South Africa believed in self-determination for the individual and different peoples of South West Africa. (Dr Waldheim had previously also made clear this basic difference in approach between South Africa and the United Nations.)

At the end of July the Secretary General released a report in New York for consideration by the Security Council of his discussions with South Africa. Dr Waldheim envisaged further contact with South Africa through a personal representative and early in October announced that Dr A. M. Escher, a retired Swiss diplomat, would visit South Africa (as his personal representative) to continue talks with Mr Vorster on the question of self-determination of South West Africa. Dr Escher arrived on October 8. Following discussions with Mr Vorster he met with various ethnic groups and political associations in South West Africa. He returned to New York on November 2, after spending 17 days in the territory.

On November 20th the Prime Minister said at a special press conference in Pretoria that he and Dr Escher had reached an agreement which constituted a framework for future political development of South West Africa. Dr Escher's report would form part of the Secretary General's report to the Security Council in December but even if the framework was rejected by the Security Council of the U.N., then he would nonetheless consider adopting it as a basis for political development of the territory. Mr Vorster made it clear that under the Government's present policy South West Africa as a whole could ultimately be completely independent from South Africa. The Prime Minister also said that the ultimate form of government in the territory could possibly be a federation, confederation or each ethnic community could decide to "go-it-alone" just as they prefer. He repeatedly stressed that under the policy of self-determination neither the United Nations nor the South African government could prescribe to the people of South West Africa what their ultimate form of government should be. "I have stated throughout — also to Dr Escher — that it is the peoples themselves who must decide," Mr Vorster said. He referred questioners to a paragraph of his signed agreement with Dr Escher which stated that experience in self-government was an essential element for eventual self-determination and that this could best be done on a regional basis. In the Escher agreement the Prime Minister also stated that he would establish an Advisory Council for South West Africa drawn from representatives of the various regions, regional governments or regional authorities.

The Secretary General submitted his report (in which the Escher-Vorster agreement was incorporated) to the Security Council on November 16. On December 7 the Security Council approved continued contacts with South Africa over the future of South West Africa but stressed that these must be conducted in the light of U.N. insistence on independence for the territory as a whole. The resolution introduced by Argentina was adopted by 13 votes to none, with Russia abstaining and China continuing her policy of "non-participation" in votes on the question. The resolution authorises Dr Waldheim to "continue his valuable efforts" to seek a solution and to report back to the council not later than April 30 1973.

Another important international event was the state visit to Malawi in March by the South African President, Mr J. J. Fouché. It was the first such visit to an independent Black African State by a South African Head of State. (The Malawian President, Dr Kamuzu Banda, visited South Africa in 1971.) Mr Fouché was accompanied by the Minister for Foreign Affairs, Dr H. Muller and the Secretary for Foreign Affairs, Mr B. G. Fourie. At the Malawi state banquet held in honour of President Fouché, Dr Banda reaffirmed his country's policy of continued dialogue with South Africa and he expressed again his opposition to other African states who favoured violence or boycotts in order to force social change in South Africa.

South Africa's relations with Rhodesia also came under the spotlight when Britain's Pearce Commission in May found the agreement reached between the British and Rhodesian governments to break to constitutional deadlock not acceptable to the Black Rhodesian community. The South African Prime Minister, Mr Vorster said in Cape Town that this conclusion had not made matters easier for the governments of Southern Africa but that South Africa's relations with and its attitude towards Britain and Rhodesia were in no way changed by the commission's report. Mr Vorster was critical of the way in which the Pearce Commission set about its task.

Other notable events with an international flavour included the following: The death of five South African policemen on border duty in the Eastern Caprivi Strip; The despatch of the first Black police to Caprivi; On September 27 the United Nations General Assembly's Committee dealing with trusteeship and non-selfgoverning territories voted 78 to 13 to seat members of Black African terrorist movements operating in Southern Africa as observers. The Republic of South Africa objected to this step as being a clear violation of the United Nations Charter; On June 28 President Nixon's top official on Africa, Assistant Secretary of State for Africa, David Newson, said in a prepared speech in Chicago that there has not been a softening of U.S. policy towards South Africa since Mr. Nixon took office in 1969; South African Airways pilots participated in a one-day world wide strike in June to focus world attention on the deadly

seriousness of the hi-jacking menace. The airline experienced its first hi-jacking on May 24.

Headlines were also made in September by the establishment of the Economic Development Bank for Equatorial and Southern Africa, by the South African industrialist-financier, Dr Anton Rupert. The bank would not only assist developing states in Africa but also Black homelands in the Republic of South Africa.

The Ovambo (South West Africa) government issued a statement on June 26 that the South African government had agreed to their request for self-government. The agreement included a partially elected Legislative Council, a Cabinet of Ministers and an own flag and national anthem for Ovambo. When the Secretary General of the United Nations visited Ovambo early in 1972 the Executive Council of the Ovambo made it clear to him that they did not see themselves part of a unitary state for South West Africa.

Iran's (Persia's) Minister of Culture, Mr M. Pahlbold travelled to South Africa in February to open a monument to Shah Reza the Great in Johannesburg. Other visits which made news included, *inter alia,* that of Admiral Edward Ashmore, Supreme Commander of the British Navy; C. Clyde Ferguson, U.S. Deputy Assistant Secretary of State for African Affairs; Her Royal Highness the Infanta Pilar of Spain; Aristotele Onassis of Greece and the Governor General of Mocambique and Mrs dos Santos. Chief Gatsha Buthelezi, Chief Executive Officer of the Zulu homeland and Chief Kaiser Matanzima of the Transkei went to the U.S.A. Chief Buthelezi also visited Malawi. A notable first was the visit of the Zulu King, Paramount Chief Zwelithine Bhekuzulu to New York to open a show of African arts and crafts.

PEOPLE, PLACES AND EVENTS

Celebration: Dorothy Fisher, South Africa's longest surviving heart transplant patient, celebrated her third anniversary with a new heart.

Visitors: Personalities from all walks of life visited the Republic. They included the Lama of Tibet, the Patriarch of Alexandria, Dame Margot Fonteyn of ballet fame, tragedienne Aleka Katseli from Greece, and Cantor Moshe Stern from America.

Deaths: The "father" of the South African Air Force and the first man to fly from Britain to South Africa, Sir Pierre van Ryneveld; legendary Xhosa millionaire herbalist and father of more than 200 children, Khotso Sethuntsa.

Heroes: Police sergeant J. W. Fouché was awarded the Police Star of Merit for saving the lives of 104 people trapped by floods; the "Miners' VC" for bravery went to miner Macaki Ndzondzwana.

Records: The world's "biggest" collision at sea occurred off the southern Cape shore; not far away, a world record long-fin tunny fish was boated.

SPORT AND RECREATION

Perhaps the outstanding sporting achievement of the year was the Republic's first ever victory in the Federation Cup tennis tournament. What made the success even more exciting was the fact that it was achieved on home soil — the first time that the world's top international tournament for women tennis was held in South Africa.

There were other notable achievements. Athlete Dicky Broberg was awarded the Helms Trophy Award for the Continent of

Africa; golfer Gary Player was acclaimed sportsman of the decade after victories in the United States PGA championship and the Piccadilly World Series in Britain; Bob Hewitt and Frew McMillan showed why they have been one of the world's most successful men's tennis doubles pairs ever, by winning the Wimbledon title for the second time.

ECONOMIC AFFAIRS

Currency matters dominated the economic and financial scene during 1972. On June 30 the acting Minister of Finance, Mr S. L. Muller announced that the Rand would remain linked with the pound sterling, floating in tandem against the major world currencies. His statement follows on the British decision to let the pound float. In December 1971, in the general re-alignment of currencies, the Rand was pegged 12,28 per cent below its previous parity. That adjustment narrowed the margin which existed when sterling devalued by 14 per cent in 1967, the Rand remaining unchanged. (In terms of the US dollar the Rand was then devalued by about 4 per cent.) The June (1972) statement became an effective devaluation of the Rand of 5 per cent on the December 1971 level. While the link with sterling was retained, the dollar therefore became nearly 10 per cent more expensive than before the 1971 currency crisis. Four months later, on October 24, the Minister of Finance, Dr N. J. Diederichs, announced a formal devaluation of the Rand by 4,2 per cent and a severing of the Rand's link with the downward plunging "floating" pound sterling. Since sterling had dropped by more than 8 per cent on the December 1971 level the decision to devalue formally in fact represented a 4 per cent recovery in the formal value of the Rand on the international market. Dr Diederichs also announced that the Rand would in future be tied to the US dollar.

The budget presented to Parliament by Finance Minister Diederichs set new records in estimated expenditure (R2,8 billion) and income at about the same level with an expected surplus of income over expenditure of R2,7 million.

The general economic picture for 1972 indicated that an upswing was in the making and a moderate economic revival was

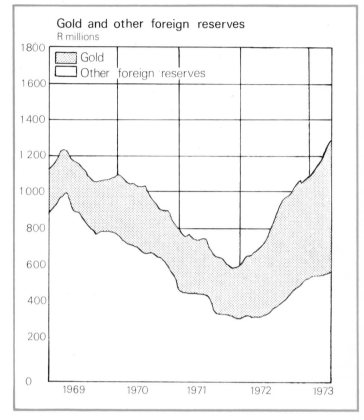

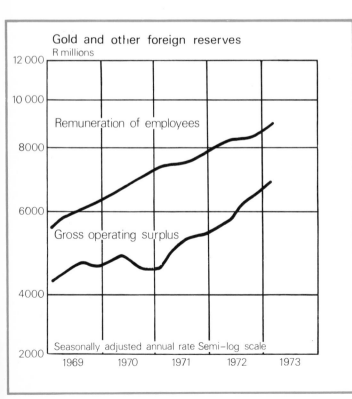

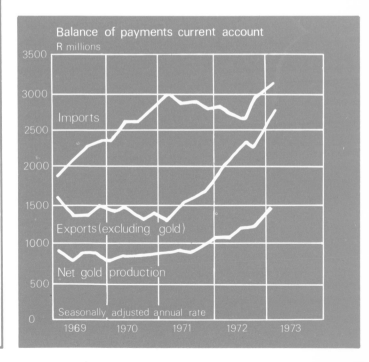

observed in the last quarter. At the end of the year the value of share trading on the Johannesburg Stock Exchange showed an almost 100 per cent improvement on 1971 topping R1 100 million on a volume of 550 million shares. Improved Rand earnings arising out of devaluation, big increases in overseas sales of agricultural products (the gross value of agricultural production for the season 1971/72 reached a record R1 625 million) and an upturn in world demand for platinum, wool, sugar, and diamonds, led to a spurt in exports while import controls (on July 24 the Minister of Economic Affairs, Mr S. L. Muller announced a moderate relaxation of import controls) and the effect of devaluation led to a decrease in imports, thus cutting the adverse balance of trade by R559 million. Gold sales increased from R763 million in 1971 to a record R1 090 million. The Republic's reserves at the end of 1972 was double that of January 1971.

Some highlights in the economic recovery was the news in July that Rustenburg Platinum Mines had landed a contract with Ford Motor Company of the US worth R140 million in three years, to supply Ford with platinum for manufacturing exhaust-gas convertors, an anti-pollution device. In September General Motors signed a contract with Impala Platinum for 300 000 ounces of platinum per year and 120 000 ounces of palladium. The contract enabled Impala to launch production expansion costing R75 million. Natal Associated Collieries announced in August that it had entered into a R25 million agreement for the supply of coal to Nord Deutsche Kraft Werke. The new East Driefontein gold mine which cost R60 million was officially opened by Mr A. Louw, Chairman of Gold Fields. Tourists to South Africa topped half a million for the first time earning the country nearly R80 million in foreign exchange. In August the Steel and Engineering Industries Federation of South Africa announced that capital investment for 1972 would reach a record R400 million, twice as much as in 1971. On July 19 the Postmaster-General, Mr Louis Rive, signed a loan with Deutsche Bank, Luxembourg, for R65 million to be used in telecommunications capital improvements totalling R139 million. (This was the first loan by the Post Office since becoming autonomous.) The previous day, July 18, the Minister of Finance, Dr Nic Diederichs, signed an agreement in London with Western Bank Ltd for a 50 million dollar Euro-currency loan. The Iron and Steel Corporation (ISCOR) announced on June 3 that it had reached an agreement with Voest, Austria's largest steel producer, to set up jointly a R350 million works to produce semi-processed steel products for export. The works will be sited on the new Sishen-Saldanha railway line. Shortly afterwards, in August, a decision was taken in principle by the Industrial Development Corporation to build a R20 million dry dock at Saldanha.

On December 1 South Africa's railway workers received a R100 million rise in wages — a rise of approximately 15 per cent. The government also announced in December that it was offering a 25 per cent tax concession to industrialists who wanted to move their plants from the existing Pretoria-Johannesbrug-Vereeniging triangle to areas bordering on Black homelands in order to provide employment for the homelands, speed up development in the homelands and border areas and to relieve the burden on existing infrastructural services in the triangle.

The South African Broadcasting Corporation unveiled a model of its new R30 million television and radio-complex to be constructed in Auckland Park, Johannesburg. The Prime Minister officially opened the largest urban road tunnel in Africa, the Daspoort tunnel, Pretoria, on August 10. The Carlton Hotel,

a landmark in Johannesburg, was opened by Mr Harry Oppenheimer on November 21. Shipyards in Cape Town tackled their biggest job ever when repairs began on the gaping hole in the 95 000 ton Liberian tanker *Oswego Gaurdian* after its collision with the Greek oil carrier *Texanita* off the coast of South Africa in July. Another giant offshore drilling rig arrived in Cape Town in September to join in the search for oil. The R7,5 million rig Sedco 135 will operate in the Caltex concession area off the South-east coast of the Cape province.

The Minister of Transport, Mr Schoeman, officially opened the new Jan Smuts international air terminal built at a cost of R32 million. What is generally recognised by experts as the world's finest passenger train, the new Blue Train, made its first scheduled run from Pretoria to Cape Town on September 4.

The link-up of the two centre sections of the 82 kilometre Orange-Fish tunnel, part of the mammoth Orange River Hydro-Electric Project, was completed in June.

South African Airways announced it was planning to purchase two more Boeing Jumbo Jets to bring the airline's Jumbo fleet to five. South African Airways also announced a pool agreement with the Brazilian Airline, Varig, and the introduction of a new route, with BOAC, between South Africa and the Far East.

In January a Brazilian trade mission, led by the President of the Bank of Brazil, followed by one from Taiwan, was the first foreign trade mission to arrive in South Africa. The French trade mission which arrived in February was unique in that it consisted of seven high ranking members of the French Senate.

South African Railways made history in February when the first super carrier train was unveiled in Kimberley. The train is almost 1,6 kilometres long and with its seven diesel locomotives can transport an ore load of nearly 12 000 metric tons.

The 10th international symposium on the application of computer methods in the mineral industry was held in Johannesburg from April 9 to April 14.

In November the government's Department of Industries announced that the number of models of automobiles assembled in the Republic were to be cut down. (There are 50 different models for sale.) The main object was to rationalise the car industry, help assemblers to reach the 67 per cent local content by weight required in 1976 for tariff barrier protection and tax rebates. The National Transport Commission's Chief Engineer (planning) announced in May that more than R1 billion would be spent in the next 10 years to expand the country's dual carriage road system. The Italian Company Alfa Romeo announced that it would invest R10 million in South Africa to increase production and in December General Motors produced its millionth motor vehicle at the Port Elizabeth assembly line.

Alusaf, the aluminium producer at Richards Bay announced plans in July to expand production at a cost of R15 million.

The Chairman of the Electricity Supply Commission Dr R. L. Straszacker announced in Johannesburg that South Africa's first nucleur power station would be operational at Koeberg near Cape Town in September 1981.

A new monthly magazine for Black businessmen titled "African Business and Chamber of Commerce Review" saw the light in October.

The diversity of South Africa's economy was illustrated by the export of a thousand pianos to Europe while German, French, British and Chilean firms placed tentative orders for a South African made snow plow. A South African machine capable of laying 4 000 bricks per day won a gold medal at the International Exhibition of Inventions and Techniques in Geneva.

LOOKING BACK IMPORTANT SOUTH AFRICAN HISTORICAL EVENTS

1485 Diego Cao landed at Cape Cross north of Walvis Bay.

1488 Bartholomew Diaz discovered the Cape.

1497 On November 26 Vasco da Gama anchored at Mossel Bay. On Christmas Day, 1497, Vasco da Gama discovered Natal.

1580 Francis Drake sighted the Cape.

1652 On April 6, Jan van Riebeeck landed at the Cape and formed the first settlement.

1657 First Free Burghers.

1658 About 400 slaves imported from West Africa.

1679 Stellenbosch founded by Simon van der Stel.

1685 Copper discovered in Namaqualand.

1688 Arrival of the first Huguenot settlers.

1774 First mission station in South Africa, at Genadendal, established by George Schmidt of the Moravian Mission Society.

1778 The Fish River made the Eastern boundary.

1779 Xhosas who crossed the Fish River and invaded the Cape Colony, repelled in the First Kaffir War.

1782 First issue of paper rixdollars. Wreck of the *Grosvenor*.

1789 First official overseas mail service.

1795-1803 First British occupation of the Cape.

1803-06 Cape returned to Batavian Republic.

1806 Second occupation of the Cape by Britain.

1814 Holland ceded the Cape to Britain.

1819 Cape boundary extended to Keiskamma River.

1820 Arrival of 5 000 British settlers.

1826 The first vocabulary of a South African Bantu Language (Xhosa) published by the missionary John Bennie.

1827 First South African Medical Society formed, at Cape Town.

1828 Death of the Zulu despot Chaka. English becomes the official language.

1829 University of Cape Town opened.

1834 Slavery abolished. First grammar of a South African Bantu language (Xhosa) written by William B. Boyce; published by the Wesleyan Mission Press, Grahamstown.

1835 Durban founded. Beginning of the Trichardt Trek.

1836 Great Trek from the Cape.

1838 Retief's treaty with Dingaan. Massacre of Boers under Retief by Dingaan. Andries Pretorius won battle of Blood River. Dingaan overthrown. Republic of Natal founded.

1843 Natal proclaimed a British colony.

1844 Majority of Voortrekkers left Natal.

1848 British sovereignty proclaimed between Orange and Vaal Rivers.

1852 Britain recognised independence of Transvaal in Sand River Convention.

1854 Britain recognised independence of Orange Free State in Convention of Bloemfontein

1860 The first railway, a link of two miles between the Point and Port Natal, opened to traffic. First stretch of telegraph line, between Cape Town and Simonstown, in operation. Lighthouse built at Cape Point — then highest in world. First importation of labourers from India for sugar plantations in Natal. Inauguration of Cape Town docks. October 26, first weather service established.

1867 First diamond discovered near Hopetown.

1868 Basutoland annexed by Britain.

1869 Diamonds discovered near Kimberley.

1870 Diamond fields annexed by Britain. Gold discovered in Murchison range.

1872 Parliamentary government granted to Cape Colony.

1873 Gold discovered in Lydenburg district.

1877 Transvaal proclaimed British territory.

1880 Formation of Afrikaner Bond. First Anglo-Boer War.

1881 Transvaal regained independence under British suzerainty. Use of Afrikaans in Cape Parliament permitted. Electric lighting installed in Adderley Street, Cape Town.

1882 First telephone exchange opened May 1, at Port Elizabeth. Kimberley the first urban community in Southern Africa to introduce electricity.

1883 Paul Kruger President of South African Republic.

1884 Barberton goldfields opened. Treaty of London (February 27) granted Transvaal full independence with exception of treaties with foreign states. Basutoland Crown Protectorate.

1885 Bechuanaland British Protectorate. Railway Cape Town-Kimberley opened.

1886 Johannesburg founded. Opening of Witwatersrand gold fields.

1890 Cecil Rhodes Prime Minister of the Cape.

1892 Railway Cape Town-Johannesburg completed.

1895 Jameson Raid. Annexation of Bechuanaland to Cape Colony.

1896 Surrender and trial of Jameson.

1897 Railway opened from Cape Town to Bulawayo.

1898 Paul Kruger elected fourth time as President.

1899-1902 War between Great Britain and the two Boer Republics.

1902 Peace of Vereeniging (May 31). Transvaal and Orange Free State British colonies. Death of Cecil Rhodes. Founding of Premier Diamond Mine.

1904 Death of ex-President Kruger at Clarens, Switzerland.

1906 Self-government granted to the Transvaal.

1907 Orange River Colony granted self-government.

1908 National Convention in Durban, further meetings in 1909 in Cape Town and Bloemfontein. The small laboratory established by the Government of the South African Republic at Daspoort for Arnold Theiler moved to Onderstepoort. This was the beginning of the Division of Veterinary Services.

1909 South Africa Act passed by Imperial Parliament.

1910 Constitution of the Union of South Africa, May 31. Louis Botha first Prime Minister.

1913 General Hertzog formed National Party. Miners' strike and riots on Witwatersrand. Indian riots in Natal. March of Natal Indians into Transvaal. National Botanical gardens established at Kirstenbosch. December 16, unveiling of National Women's Monument at Bloemfontein in memory of 26 370 Afrikaner women and children who died in concentration camps during Anglo-Boer War.

1914 Industrial disturbances on Witwatersrand. Income tax introduced. Outbreak of First World War, August 4. Parliament, on September 10, decided with 91 against 12 votes in favour of participation in war. Outbreak of the Rebellion. Martial Law proclaimed. Military expedition to South West Africa.

1916 Expeditionary Force to German East Africa under command of General Smuts.

1918 November 11, Armistice. Serious influenza epidemic.

1919 South Africa granted Mandate over South West Africa. Death of General Botha. General Smuts Prime Minister.

1920   First successful flight Cairo to Cape by Sir Pierre van Ryneveld, and Sir Quintin Brand.

1922   General Strike followed by widespread revolutionary movements in mining districts. Martial Law. Southern Rhodesia voted against General Smuts' offer to join South Africa.

1923   18th December, first radio broadcast in South Africa.

1924   General Hertzog Prime Minister.

1925   Afrikaans second official language. Discovery of rich platinum deposits. South Africa back on gold standard. Visit by Prince of Wales.

1926   General Hertzog at Imperial Conference in London. Dominions granted equal legal status with Britain.

1927   Flag Agreement, the orange-white-blue tricolour and the Union Jack becoming the official flags. Parliament approved of establishment of South African iron and steel industry. Department of External Affairs established. Beam radio communications with Great Britain.

1931   Statute of Westminster passed by Imperial Parliament.

1932   Wireless telephone communication with Britain. On December 29, South Africa abandoned gold standard.

1933   Coalition Government of National and South African Parties, under General Hertzog as Prime Minister. First Afrikaans Bible issued.

1934   Jonker diamond, weighing 726 carats, found at Elandsfontein and sold for R140 000.

1936   Passing of Representation of Natives Act. South African Broadcasting Corporation established. Empire Exhibition in Johannesburg.

1938   Centenary celebrations of Great Trek. Foundation stone laid for Voortrekker Monument at Pretoria. *Die Stem van Suid-Afrika* and *God Save the King* adopted as national anthems.

1939   General Smuts Prime Minister. On September 6, Parliament, with 80 votes against 67, decided to enter war against Germany.

1943   General Smuts Prime Minister.

1945   End of hostilities. Beginning of South Africa's remarkable industrial development.

1948   Dr. D. F. Malan Prime Minister.

1949   Serious rioting in Durban by Zulus against Indians. Voortrekker Monument unveiled. Devaluation of sterling.

1950   Appeal to Privy Council abolished. September 11, death of Field-Marshal Smuts. South African Air Force squadron for Korean war.

1952   Tercentenary celebrations of arrival of Jan van Riebeeck and establishment of first White settlement in Cape.

1954   Mr J. G. Strijdom Prime Minister.

1955   First petrol produced from coal.

1956   Unprecedented activity in South African ports as a result of closure of Suez Canal.

1957   Simonstown Naval Base officially handed over to South African Government. As from April 6 — Van Riebeeck Day — South Africa Flag hoisted as only flag on all Government buildings. May 3, Die Stem van Suid-Afrika only National Anthem.

1958   August 23, death of the Prime Minister, Adv. J. G. Strijdom. September 2, Dr H. F. Verwoerd chosen as Prime Minister. December 10, the South African Cabinet decides to introduce decimal coinage in 1961.

1959   February 7, death of Dr Daniël F. Malan — Prime Minister from 1948 until his retirement in 1954 — at age of 84.

1960   January 20, Dr Verwoerd announced Referendum plan. February 3, British Prime Minister Macmillan addresses members of both Houses of Parliament in Cape Town. April 9, attempted assassination of Prime Minister Dr Verwoerd. October 5, republican referendum.

1961   March 15, Dr Verwoerd withdraws South Africa's application for continued membership of the Commonwealth. May 31, Republic of South Africa established. Mr C. R. Swart first State President.

1962   January 23, Prime Minister Dr H. F. Verwoerd announced in Parliament that Government will grant self-government to the Transkei.

1963   Transkei achieves self-government.

1964   New nickel coinage for South Africa. Coloureds' Representative Council to be formed.

1965   Atlas Aircraft Corporation formed on Witwatersrand to establish new South African aircraft industry.

1966   March 30, General Election — National Party returned to power with biggest majority in South Africa's political history; May 31, fifth anniversary of the Republic of South Africa; July 18, World Court rejects complaints brought by Ethiopia and Liberia against South African rule over South West Africa; September 6, Dr. H. F. Verwoerd, Prime Minister since 1958, assassinated in the House of Assembly by Dimitri Tsafendas, a Parliamentary messenger; September 13, Mr B. J. Vorster becomes Prime Minister.

1967   In January, Mr Vorster held discussions in Cape Town with Chief Leabua Jonathan, Prime Minister of Lesotho. South Africa promised technical and economic aid to Lesotho; in December Professor Chris Barnard's performed heart transplant on Mr Louis Washkansky.

1968   January 2, Professor Barnard performs second heart transplant. The recipient was Dr Philip Blaiberg, 58, of Cape Town; April, Mr J. J. Fouché sworn in as State President.

1970   A population census, the first for 10 years, was taken, indicating that the population might exceed 21 000 000 when final figures are known. The Prime Minister, Mr John Vorster, embarked on an overseas tour and later visited Malawi. Development of new uranium enrichment process by South African scientists.

1971   Internal self-government granted to Zulu nation. State visit by President Banda of Malawi.

1972   U.N. Secretary General Kurt Waldheim visits Republic; three further Black Homelands, Bophuthatswana, the Ciskei and Lebowa, attain status of self-governing territories within the Republic of South Africa.

3

Politics and government

Cape Town, legislative capital of South Africa. The Houses of Parliament is situated at the lower left end of the 320 year old public gardens seen here in the right centre of the aerial photograph of South Africa's mother city.

Restoration of the "Tuynhuys" (Garden Home) official residence of the State President in Cape Town was completed in 1972. The original residence, erected as a guest house for V.I.P.'s, was completed 290 years ago. The photo shows part of the interior of the house.

Photo: S.A. Digest

On July 31 the South African Prime Minister announced extensive changes in his Cabinet. The outgoing Ministers were D. C. H. Uys (Agriculture), F. W. Waring (Sport and Indian Affairs), Dr C. de Wet (Mines and Health), B. Coetzee (Community Development), and T. J. A. Gerdener (Interior). The newcomers were A. H. du Plessis, Dr P. G. J. Koornhof, H. Schoeman, Dr S. W. van der Merwe, and Prof. O. P. F. Horwood. Five new Deputy Ministers were also appointed: J. C. Heunis, J. T. Kruger, T. N. H. Janson, J. J. Malan, and J. W. Rall.

The photograph was taken shortly after the new Cabinet was sworn in by the State President.

Front row: Mr S. L. Muller, Minister of Economic Affairs and of Police; Mr M. C. Botha, Minister of Bantu Administration and Development and of Bantu Education; Dr H. Muller, Minister of Foreign Affairs; Dr N. Diederichs, Minister of Finance; the Prime Minister, Mr B. J. Vorster; the State President, Mr J. J. Fouché; Mr B. J. Schoeman, Minister of Transport; Mr P. W. Botha, Minister of Defence; Mr M. Viljoen, Minister of Labour and of Posts and Telegraphs; Mr P. C. Pelser, Minister of Justice and of

Prisons and Mr S. P. Botha, Minister of Water Affairs and of Forestry. Back row: Mr J. J. Malan, Deputy Minister of Agriculture; Mr J. T. Kruger, Deputy Minister of Police, of the Interior and of Social Welfare and Pensions; Mr J. C. Heunis, Deputy Minister of Finance and of Economic Affairs; Prof. O. P. F. Horwood, Minister of Indian Affairs and of Tourism; Mr H. Schoeman, Minister of Agriculture; Mr A. H. du Plessis, Minister of Public Works and of Community Development; Sen. J. P. van der Spuy, Minister of National Education; Dr C. P. Mulder, Minister of Information, of the Interior and of Social Welfare and Pensions; Mr J. J. Loots, Minister of Planning and of Statistics; Dr P. G. J. Koornhof, Minister of Mines, of Immigration and of Sport and Recreation; Dr S. W. van der Merwe, Minister of Health and of Coloured Relations and Rehoboth Affairs; Mr A. J. Raubenheimer, Deputy Minister of Bantu Development; Mr J. W. Rall, Deputy Minister of Transport and Mr T. N. H. Janson, Deputy Minister of Bantu Administration and Education.

Photo: Pretoria News

Although the new R10 million 30-storey Department of the Interior building in Pretoria will only be completed next year, the first personnel have already moved in. A giant computer, which will process the statistics of every person in South Africa, is already housed in the building.

Photo: Nasionale Koerante, Cape Town
In January, in preparation for the opening of the South African Parliament's annual session in Cape Town, the Cabinet gathered for the first time in the new H. F. Verwoerd Building, situated opposite the Parliament Building. The Cabinet Room is on the eighteenth floor of the tower-building. The parliamentary staff of the various government departments are housed in the new building.

Photo: The Pretoria News
The Minister of Water Affairs, Mr S. P. Botha (seated), signs the R7,9-million contract for the mechanical control equipment of the P. M. K. le Roux Dam, the second largest dam in South Africa. The largest dam, the giant Hendrik Verwoerd Dam — already completed, and the P. M. K. le Roux Dam are at the heart of the vast Orange River hydro-electric project which will eventually stretch over more than a thousand kilometres and affect an area twice the size of the United Kingdom. The 107 metres high, 765 metres long wall of the P. M. K. le Roux Dam is expected to be completed by the end of 1976.

Photo: Africamera
The newly appointed Deputy Minister of Bantu Administration and Education, Mr T. N. H. Janson (right) being welcomed by Mr J. Ramaite (left), member of the Soweto Urban Bantu Council. Mr Janson was paying his first official visit to the black township of Soweto, near Johannesburg.

Photo: Hoofstad

In a surprise announcement at the Transvaal National Party congress in Pretoria, the Minister of Transport, Mr Ben Schoeman, said that he would not make himself available as Transvaal leader and that in two years' time he would not stand again for election to Parliament. The Minister of Information and of the Interior, Dr C. P. Mulder, was then elected by an overwhelming majority as the new Transvaal leader. The photograph shows Mr Schoeman (left) congratulating Dr Mulder on his election.

Photo: Rapport

Mr Theo Gerdener, Minister of the Interior and leader of the National Party in Natal, resigned from the Cabinet and later gave up his leadership of the province and parliamentary seat to head a new organisation, Action South and Southern Africa. The purpose of the new organisation is to promote goodwill and seek co-operation between all race groups, black and white, in Southern Africa on a common basis of anti-communism.

The photograph shows Mr and Mrs Gerdener at the time of his resignation as member of the South African Cabinet.

Photos: S.A. Digest
Mr F. G. Barrie, Secretary for Information, took up the post of Controller and Auditor General — the top post in the Republic's Public Service. His successor as Secretary for Information, Dr E. M. Rhoodie (right), served from 1956 to 1971 with the Department of Information, including postings in Canberra, Washington, New York and The Hague, before becoming Assistant Editor of the international news magazine, To The Point.

Photo: The Friend
Sir De Villiers Graaff, Leader of the Opposition, being welcomed by students on his arrival at the Bloemfontein City Hall to open the 25th Free State provincial congress of the United Party.

Photo: Perskor
With no less than six by-elections — four on the same day — and a mixture of urban and rural constituencies, 1972 witnessed something of a mini general election. Except for Klip River (Natal), where its majority was slashed from 1 479 to a bare 232, the ruling National Party easily retained the Caledon, Malmesbury, Johannesburg West, Vereeniging and Wakkerstroom seats. Former Springbok rugby captain, Dawie de Villiers (shown with his wife, Susanne), increased the National Party majority in Johannesburg West.

Photo: S.A. Police
Among visitors to the South African Police College in Pretoria were 52 German police officers and their wives from Berlin. The party was on a private tour of the Republic. The photograph shows some of the visitors at the Police Dog-training School.

Photo: S.A. Police
A passing-out parade with a difference. A hundred and two members of the fairer sex graduated from the Police College in Pretoria and entered service as South Africa's first women police.

Photo: Africamera
A crowd of three thousand people gathered at the new police headquarters in Soweto, the complex of Black townships near Johannesburg, for its official opening by the Minister of Police, Mr S. L. Muller. The Minister also presented 66 Black policemen with medals for exemplary conduct and faithful service to the residents of Soweto.

Photo: The Argus, Cape Town

The Indian community of South Africa is larger than all the other Indian communities of Africa combined. It is the policy of the South African Government to maintain close contact with the various population groups. Here members of the executive committee of the South African Indian Council are seen with the Minister of Indian Affairs, Mr F. E. Waring (second from left), and the Prime Minister, Mr B. J. Vorster (fourth from left). These discussions were held at the beginning of the year in Cape Town. The members of the executive committee are (from left): Mr H. E. Joosub, Mr A. M. Rajab (chairman), Dr M. B. Naidoo, Mr J. N. Reddy, and Mr Y. S. Chinsamy.

Photo: Africamera

There was a shock leadership upset within the opposition United Party, with Mr Harry Schwarz, a member of the Transvaal Provincial Council, deposing Mr Marais Steyn, M.P., as Transvaal leader of the Party. The photograph shows sir De Villiers Graaff, Leader of the Opposition, at the Transvaal congress of his party, together with Mr Schwarz (left) and Mr Marais Steyn (right).

Photo: S.A Digest

When the members of the Transkeian Cabinet visited Cape Town as guests of the South African Government, they were taken on a short cruise on Table Bay. The Chief Minister of South Africa's first Bantu Homeland to achieve self-government, Paramount Chief Kaiser Matanzima, obviously enjoyed handling the tugboat Danie Malan, while Captain Eric Davis looked on.

Photo: Perskor

Two more black Homelands achieved the status of self-governing territories within the Republic, each with his own Cabinet and Legislative Assembly. The Homelands of the Tswana people and North Sotho people become the territories of Bophuthatswana and Lebowa, respectively. The other two self-governing territories are the Transkei and the Ciskei. The South African Minister of Bantu Development, Mr M. C. Botha (photo), is in charge of South African Government policy, which envisages self-determination for each of the Republic's black nations.

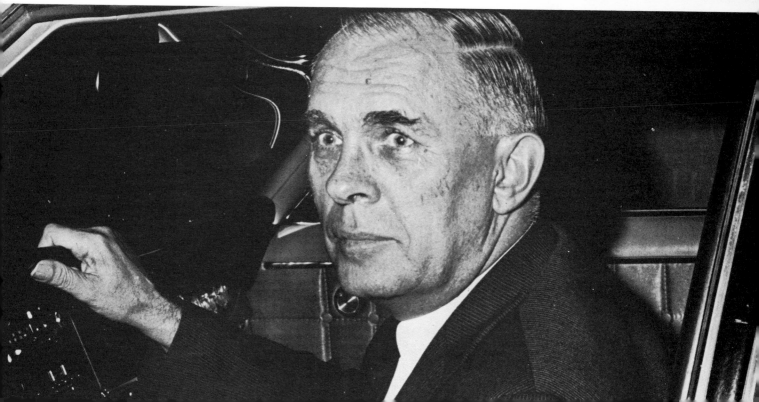

Photo: Perskor

In keeping with his practice of having frequent discussions with representatives of all the diverse population groups of the Republic, the Prime Minister (fourth from right) received a delegation of the Elected Council of Damaraland (South West Africa) for extensive talks. Also present was the Minister of Foreign Affairs, Dr H. Muller (third from right)

Photo: Die Burger

The Chairman of the Coloured Persons' Representative Council, Mr Tom Schwartz, chatting to the Chief of the South African Defence Force, Admiral H. H. Biermann, the head of Defence Administration, lieutenant-general H. P. Laubscher (left), and the head of the army, lieutenant-general W. P. Louw (right).
Earlier the Minister of Defence, Mr P. W. Botha, announced the establishment of a new prestige unit, the Coloured Corps Special Service Battalion. The new unit would be geared to train and equip Coloured trainees and enable them eventually to contribute efficiently to the defence of the Republic.

Photo: Paratus

South Africa's new hydrographic survey ship, SAS Protea, arrives in Simonstown at the completion of its maiden voyage from Britain. The ship was built in Scotland at a cost of R6-million.

Photo: S.A. Digest

On June 1, the Tswana Homeland was accorded the status of a self-governing territory within the Republic of South Africa. The territory adopted the name of *Bophuthatswana*.

The development reaffirmed the South African Government's declared intention of leading the various black nations of South Africa to self-government and eventual independence. The photograph shows Chief Lucas Mangope (standing), first Chief Minister of the new self-governing territory, with his cabinet. From the left: Mr J. B. Toto, Minister of Justice, Chief M. Setlogelo, Minister of Education, Chief H. T. Maseloane, Minister of Community Affairs, Mr D. P. Kgotleng, Minister of Works, and Chief S. G. Ntuane, Minister of Agriculture.

On October 4, Chief Mangope's National Independence Party overwhelmly won the territory's first general election.

25

Photos: Africamera; Nasionale Koerante

The State President, Mr Jim Fouché, opened the ultra-modern submarine base SAS Drommedaris at Simonstown and stated that it was the first base of its kind in Africa. During the ceremony which was attended by many guests including the Chief of the French Navy, Admiral Mae de Joybert, South Africa's third and newest submarine, the Johanna van der Merwe (photo), was welcomed to Simonstown. Defence Minister P. W. Botha, greeting members of the crew, described the submarine's arrival as "another important step in the protection of the strategic Cape sea route".

Photos: Paratus; Die Burger

When he opened the new Atlas Aircraft Military Base, between Johannesburg and Pretoria, the Minister of Defence, Mr P. W. Botha (left) praised the role the Atlas Aircraft Corporation had played in the interest of the defence of the country since 1965. The establishment of the Corporation introduced a vast new technology into the Republic's industrial scene. The Corporation was already in the process of building more advanced planes, the Minister said. On the right is Admiral H. H. Biermann, new Chief of the Defence Force. The other photo shows Impala jets produced by Atlas in spectacular formation flight.

Photo: Paratus

Phase Two of the Republic's extensive Nassau Radar System was handed over to the Defence Force at the beginning of 1972. This includes an underground complex regarded as one of the most modern in the world — it is secure even against the shock waves of a standard atomic bomb exploding nearby. On the photograph the operation of a sophisticated camera is demonstrated to visitors attending the handing-over ceremony.

27

4

International relations

Photo: S.A. Digest
A state banquet was arranged for the Secretary General of the United Nations, Dr Kurt Waldheim, during his visit to South Africa to discuss the South West Africa issue. (See overview.) In the photograph taken in the three-century old Castle of Good Hope in Cape Town is seen, from left to right, the South African Prime Minister and Mrs B. J. Vorster, Dr Waldheim, Mrs Biermann and Admiral H. H. Biermann, Chief of Staff of the South African Defence Force.

Photo: S.A. Digest

At a special press conference in Pretoria in November, the Prime Minister replied to questions on South Africa's stand on the South West Africa issue following the submission of Dr Alfred Escher's report to the UN Secretary General, Dr Kurt Waldheim. On the Prime Minister's left is Dr C. P. Mulder, Minister of Information and Dr Eschel Rhoodie, Permanent Secretary of State for Information, Barry Jennan of the Daily News Durban, John D'Oliveira, political correspondent of The Star, Johannesburg, and Neville Krige of Radio South Africa.

Photo: Pretoria News

Dr A. Escher, personal representative of Dr Kurt Waldheim, Secretary General of the United Nations (see overview) arriving at the Union Buildings, Pretoria, for talks with the South African Prime Minister. He is seen here (right) being welcomed by Dr H. Muller, South Africa's Foreign Minister.

Photo: S.A. Panorama

The first visit by a South African Head of State to an independent Black African country began on March 17 when State President Fouché arrived in Malawi at the invitation of President Kamuzu Banda. In 1971 the Malawi President had paid a state visit to South Africa. In the photographs Mrs Fouché is handed a bouquet at Malawi's Chileka Airport and the State President is shown seated next to President Banda at a mass youth rally.

Photo: Panorama
Reza Shah, Reza the Great, of Persia (Iran) lived from 1941 to 1944 in exile in a stately house in Mountain-view, Johannesburg, where he died in 1944. He was later buried in Teheran. In January 1972 the house was proclaimed an historic museum. The photograph shows part of the entrance foyer with an oil painting of Reza the Great.

34

Photo: Africamera
The Iranian (Persia) Minister of Culture, Mr M. Pahlbold (centre) flanked by the South African Minister of Education, Senator J. P. van der Spuy (right) and the Mayor of Johannesburg Mr Alf Widman at the opening of the Reza Shah monument in Johannesburg on January 21.

Photo: S.A. Digest
The first public appearance of Premier Chiang Ching-Kuo, eldest son of President Chiang Kai-Shek, after the confirmation of his appointment of Prime Minister of the Republic of China, was his attendance at a reception given to celebrate South Africa's Republic Day on May 31. Here he toasts the South Africa Consul-General in Taipei and Mrs J. H. Selfe at the reception in the Grand Hotel.

Photo: Rand Daily Mail
The Spanish Navy's Training ship Juan Sebastian de Elcano paid a visit to South Africa in June and is seen here under full sail outside Durban.

Photo: Alan Lipschitz
Die Transvaler, Johannesburg

Another visitor to the United States (also for the first time) was Paramount Chief Kaiser Matanzima, Leader of the Government in the Transkei, home state of the Xhosa nation. He is seen here at Jan Smuts international airport being welcomed home by fellow Xhosas.

Photo: Nasionale Koerante

Chief Gatsha Buthelezi, Chief Executive Officer of the Zulu Territorial Authority, paid his first visit to America, as a guest of the US State Department. He is seen on his return, signing autographs for well wishers.

Photo: Africamera

Malawi's Ambassador to South Africa, Mr Joseph Kachingwe talks to Dr W. R. Hertzog, Chairman of the South African Foreign Trade Organisation, at a luncheon during a seminar on export opportunities to Malawi — held in Johannesburg, the first week of September.

38

Photo (a) Perskor
(b) Rennie Botha, Rapport.

South Africa experienced its first hi-jacking last year when in May, Fred Kamil and Abon Yaghi hijacked a Boeing 727 of South African Airways, just before touchdown in Johannesburg on a scheduled flight from Salisbury, Rhodesia. The hi-jacked aircraft ended up in Malawi after the pilot, Captain B. D. Flemington had deluded the hijackers who were intending to fly to Madagascar. The aircraft was kept on the runway at Malawi's Chileka international airport (Blantyre) while the hijackers haggled with the pilot, passengers, the control tower and even attempted to embroil South African business tycoon Harry Oppenheimer. Finally when all of the crew and passengers had escaped, Malawi police machine-gunned the aircraft and the hijackers surrendered. Malawi refused South Africa's request to extradiction of the hijackers and the two were finally sentenced to imprisonment in Malawi by the local High Court. In the one photograph, Fred Kamil is seen being led from gaol to the Supreme Court in Blantyre, Malawi while in the other can be seen the damage to the aircraft caused by machine gun fire of the Malawian police.

Photo: Africamera
Chinese and Russian trained terrorists based in Zambia continued to slip across the border into the Eastern Caprivi (see map) to lay landmines. For the first time Black South African policemen were also sent out to the Caprivi to combat terrorist activities. Here a group of men bare their heads in prayer before departure from Waterkloof Air Force Base near Pretoria.

Photo: Perskorporasie van S.A.
American astronauts — Donald Slayton (left) and James Lovell arrived in South Africa on June 11 for a ten day photographic safari.

Photo: Perskorporasie van S.A.
Neil Armstrong, first man to set foot on the moon, had his first close-up look of South Africa in 1972 when he and his wife came out for a short visit.
The photograph was taken at a press conference in Johannesburg.

Photo: Africamera
Admiral Sir Edward Ashmore, Commander-in-Chief on the British Fleet, visited South Africa during November as a guest of the South African Defence Force. He is seen here (left) with Vice Admiral Johnson of the South African Navy.

The Governor General of Mocambique and Mrs Primental Dos Santos seen here in discussion with South Africa's Minister of Defence and Mrs P. W. Botha, and Her Royal Highness, the Infanta Pilar of Spain (sister of Prince Juan Don Callos), flanked on the right by her husband the Duke of Badajoz and the Spanish Ambassador to South Africa, The Count of Penarubia.

Ambassador C. Clyde Ferguson, United States Deputy Assistant Secretary of the State for African Affairs.

Among the many prominent guests who visited South Africa during 1972 were: Mr Aristole Onassis, shipping magnate and owner of Olympic Airlines, seen here in Johannesburg shortly after his arrival.

Photos:
1. Africamera
2. The Pretoria News
3. S.A. Digest
4. The Pretoria News

Photo: Military Historical and
          Archival Services

The Chief of the Persian (Iranian) Defence Force, Admiral F. Rassai, was one of several prominent military leaders to visit South Africa during 1972. He is seen here with South Africa's Defence Force Chief, Admiral H. Biermann.

Photo: S.A. Panorama

Theatre-goers in Britain had their first taste of Zulu theatre when Welcome Msomi's Zulu version of Macbeth, Umabatha, was performed in London in April. Umabatha received rave reviews in the press. In the photograph members of the cast in western dress meets the South Africa Ambassador, Dr H. J. Luttig. In the other pictures the cast, this time in traditional Zulu war finery, meets H.R.H. Princess Margaret.

Photo: Nasionale Koerante Bpk.

A group of French Senators, members of the Commission of Economic Affairs of the French Senate, held discussions with South Africa's Finance Minister — Dr Nico Diederichs in Cape Town during January.

Seen here with Dr Diederichs (centre) is Senator P. Mistral (left) leader of the group and Senator M. Chauty.

Photo: Volksblad, Bloemfontein

In 1972, Lesotho had a South African judge, Mr Justice J. N. C. de Villiers, as acting Chief Justice. Here at a garden party in Maseru during May King Moshoeshoe II and his Queen (right) are seen entertaining Mr Justice de Villiers and his wife.

Photo: The Natal Mercury
The U.S. Ambassador, Mr John Hurt, presented this pedigree Texan Brahman bull to Mr Gatsha Buthelezi, Chief Executive Officer of the Zulu Territorial Authority.

Photo: S.A. Panorama
The Sixth International Conference of Hereford Cattle Breeders was held in the Kruger National Park between March 12 — 18. Some 500 breeders from 23 countries and 150 from South Africa attended the conference which is held every four years. In the photographs are Hereford breeders from Spain, Finland, Portugal, Thailand, Malawi, Brazil, the Argentine, Uruguay, New Zealand, South Africa and Australia.

Photo: Panorama
The South African Dental Association celebrated its golden jubilee with an international conference in Johannesburg attended by more than 700 dental surgeons from South Africa and many overseas countries. The South African Minister of Health, Dr S. W. van der Merwe, is seen here, delivering the opening address in the Carlton Centre, Johannesburg.

5

The economy
and communications

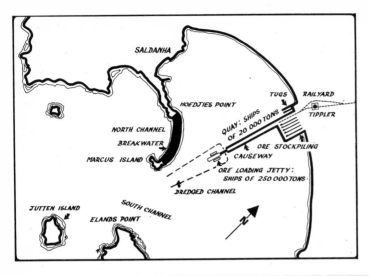

Photo: S.A. Panorama
The H. F. Verwoerd dam puts on a spectacular show as it overflows on the day of the official opening of the $70 million structure by the wife of the late Prime Minister, Mrs Betsie Verwoerd. The dam forms part of a $1,2 Billion development project to harness the river's water for agricultural and industrial use.

Photo: S.A. Digest
Final State approval was received for the Iron and Steel Corporation to proceed with the $550 million Sishen-Saldanha project. The project entails the construction of a railway of 853 kilometres long and the development of an ore export harbour. The aerial view is of Saldanha Bay while the map shows the layout of the new harbour. A new R20 million dry dock is also to be built here under the auspices of the Industrial Development Corporation.

Photo: S.A. Panorama

The most beautiful, the most modern and the finest train in the world. This is the unanimous opinion of seasoned world travellers describing South Africa's new Blue Train running between Cape Town and Johannesburg, a distance of some 1 500 kilometres. The train which cost $6,3 million to build, made its first scheduled run on September 4 from Pretoria to Cape Town.

Photo: Africamera, Johannesburg

The Governor of the South African Reserve Bank, Dr T. W. de Jongh announced the abolition of the existing ceiling on bank credit in November as the gold and foreign reserves began reaching for record heights.

Photo: Castle-Marine
The Pendennis Castle, 28 442 tons, entered Table Bay on October 4 after a voyage of 11½ days — marking the centenary of the arrival in Table Bay of the first of a long line of Castle steamers which have served South Africa.
One hundred years ago the Walmer Castle, 2 446 tons, steamed into the Cape after 25 days.

Photo: S.A. Digest
In June, the two main sections of the world's largest and longest tunnel, the 83 kilometre Orange-Fish tunnel (part of the Orange River Hydro-Electric and Irrigation Project) were linked. After the blast through, champagne flowed 300 metres below the bleak Suurberg plateau, in the north-eastern Cape Province.

Photo: Africamera, Johannesburg
Dr Nico Diederichs, Minister of Finance, signs an agreement which gives South Africa a $50 million Euro-currency loan for five years. With him at the ceremony which took place in the South African Embassy in London on July 18 is Mr Harry Schwarz, representing Western Bank Ltd. of Johannesburg.

Photo: Richard Wege, Cape Town

The Beacon Island Hotel, a spectacular setting on South Africa's east coast ("Garden Route"), opened its doors in 1972. The hotel at Plettenberg Bay, south of Port Elizabeth, is one of several international hotels recently opened to cater for South Africa's flourishing tourist trade. During 1972 nearly 500 000 tourists visited South Africa.

56

Photo: Carlton Hotel, Johannesburg

Johannesburg's massive Carlton Hotel is seen against the blood red setting of a summer evening. Its towering neighbour is the Trust Bank's Johannesburg head office. The Carlton, which opened in September is built on top of a three tier subterranean city of shops and restaurants linked with the street level by elevators and escalators.

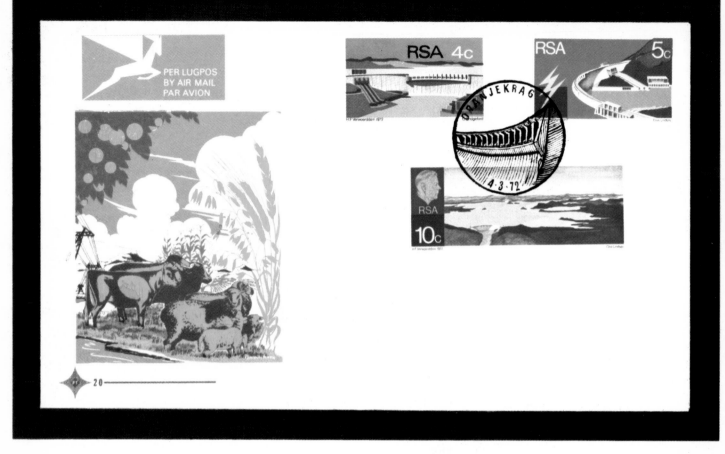

Photo: S.A. Post Office

1.   Commemorative envelope and the three special stamps issued when the Hendrik Verwoerd Dam in the Orange River irrigation and hydro-electric power project was officially inaugurated on March 4, 1972.

3. Issued on May 15, 1972 to accentuate the importance of South Africa's Wool Industry.

2. To commemorate the centenary of the Society for the Prevention of Cruelty to Animals.

Photo: The Argus, Cape Town
Trade Missions from abroad were a frequent sight during 1972. Here members of the Northern Ireland trade mission, Messrs W. C. S. Wilson and J. Attebery (leader) are seen with the British Trade Consul in Johannesburg, Mr A. Shepard (right).

Photo: Safmarine
South African Marine Corporation's new super tanker, the 266 000 ton *Sinde,* was launched in November in Japan. A sister ship to the *Kulu,* seen here in the photograph, the tanker will ferry oil from Iran to South Africa.

Photo: D. Pithey
For the first time in almost five years the Vaal Dam, second largest dam in South Africa and main water source for Johannesburg, overflowed, drawing crowds of up to 30 000 visitors per day.

Photo:
In June, South African Airways ground hostesses stepped out in their new uniforms. The new ensembles modelled against the Johannesburg sky-line by South African Airways reservation clerks Shannon Pieterse (left) and Jenet Higgo, replace the kingfisher-blue new summer uniforms.

Photo: S.A. Digest
Black businessmen from South Africa are increasingly finding time and money to travel abroad. Here at Jan Smuts international airport near Johannesburg, relatives and friends welcome back a party of 40 businessmen and their wives after a tour of Britain and Europe.

Photo: Perskorporasie van S.A.
Nine Black salesmen of a Germiston-based furniture group line up to receive a motor car each for exceeding sales targets. If the salesmen set new records in the following year they will receive the cash equivalent of a new car.

Photo: Francois J. du Rand, Pretoria
The largest urban tunnel in Africa, Pretoria's 573 metre Daspoort tunnel was opened by the Prime Minister Mr B. J. Vorster on August 10.

Photo: Nasionale Koerante
The Postmaster General Mr L. F. Rive (left) inaugurated direct dialing to West Germany in April. Looking on is the West German Ambassador to South Africa Dr E. Strätling.

Photo: Pretoria News
Women's Lib. Miss Anneliese Laier, head of the Africa section of the German Bundesbank, visited Pretoria in July to meet with senior officials of the South African Reserve Bank. She is seen here with Dr Gerhard de Kock, Deputy Governor.

Photo: Perskorporasie van S.A.
Capital investment by the metal and engineering industries reached a record of $560 million during 1972, twice the amount of the previous year, as industrial expansion in South Africa continued to increase. In the photograph a "centipede" truck carries a massive 200-ton transformer manufactured in South Africa to the Poseidon power station near Cookhouse, Cape Province.

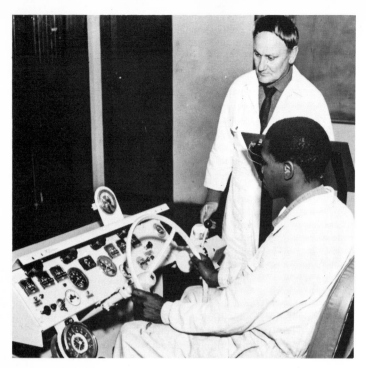

Photo: Iscor

Shortage of semi- and skilled labour has caused many companies to step up on-the-job-training. Iscor (the Iron and Steel Corporation) introduced this simulator with an instrument panel similar to that of a massive ore transporter. As in the case of aircraft simulators the model can simulate various job conditions.

Photo: S.A. Digest

Motor car trains came to South Africa in 1972 to carry as many as 600 cars, fifty per waggon. The trains, costing $1,5 million each will benefit road users and the motor industry.

Photo: Optima

The biggest breakthrough for South African platinum in the world's anti-pollution battle was announced on Sept. 21 — General Motors signed a development contract to enable Impala Platinum to supply 300 000 ounces of platinum and 120 000 ounces of palladium a year, worth about R45 million.

The agreement with Impala follows a recent arrangement between Ford, of America, and Engelhard Industries for Ford to buy up to 500 000 ounces of platinum a year if it decides to use Engelhard's platinum catalytic converters to combat air pollution.

For the first time General Motors — the world's largest car manufacturers — have acknowledged that platinum is probably the best material for exhaust mufflers and they are likely to be followed by other manufacturers, probably including Chrysler, American Motors, Japanese and German manufacturers.

The photo shows the Waterval Reduction works at Rustenburg Platina Mines.

Photo: The Star, Johannesburg

The steel headgear at President Steyn GM. It is designed to hoist 246 000 tons of rock a month from a depth of more than 2 300 m, making it the longest single-lift wind in the world.

Photos: Cloete Breytenbach, Cape Town

Sedco 135, a semi-submersible oil rig, arrived in Table Bay (Cape Town) in September 1972 for an extensive R2-million refit before commencing her task of drilling for oil off the east coast of South Africa. The project formed part of an extensive and systematic search for oil in the Republic. The Minister of Mines, Dr P. G. J. Koornhof, visited the rig (photo) and was met by Mr Sam McInnis, manager of the rig.

Photo: Africamera, Johannesburg

Dr Anton Rupert (left) Chairman of the Rembrandt Group of Companies, receives the Rand Daily Mail's 1972 Business Achievement Award from Dr Nico Diederichs, Minister of Finance. This was the first time the award was made.

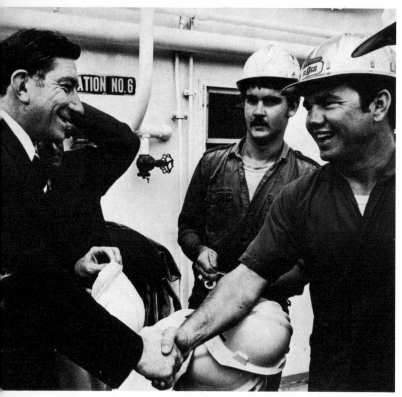

Photo: Africamera, Johannesburg

A contract for the second stage of the extensions to Table Bay Harbour, worth R18 million, was awarded in February to a consortium of Christiani and Nielsen of Cape Town and to Hollandsche Aanneming Maatschappij of Amsterdam.

(A) indicates the sea-wall being built as part of the first stage (B) the new quay wall (C) a roll-on-roll-off pier (D) a ramp for this pier (E) a launching ramp (F) a culvert (G) an existing breakwater to be removed and (H) a culvert and canal outlet for Salt River. Completion of the second stage will nearly double the capacity of the existing docks, already Africa's second busiest port after Durban.

6

Education, science
and environment

Photo: National Parks Board
Twenty Cape animal and plant species currently facing extinction were brought to the public's attention by means of a series of colour stamps issued by the Cape Province's Department of Nature Conservation.
Pictured are four of the species involved.

Photo: S.A. Panorama

The University of the Witwatersrand (Johannesburg), commonly known as "Wits", celebrated its half century of academic activities in March. With 10 000 students, Wits is the largest English language university in South Africa. The photograph shows the classic entrance to the main hall which seats more than a thousand people.

Photo: University of South Africa

The new main building of the University of South Africa (the oldest and largest correspondence institution in the world) was occupied for the first time this year and was officially inaugurated by the State President on April 14, 1973, one hundred years after the university was founded. The building overlooks Pretoria, administrative capital of South Africa. At the end of 1972 the university had almost 30 000 students and an academic -administrative staff of 1 130.

Photo: CSIR, Pretoria
The South Western Cape, including Cape Town and Saldanha Bay, as photographed for the first time by satellite from a height of 900 km. This picture forms part of a series of transparencies which were taken over South Africa from the earth resources technology satellite (ERTS) launched in June by the American National Aeronautics and Space Administration (NASA). Scores of countries, including South Africa participated in the ERTS programme.

Photo: Perskor
Mr Archer Tongue, Director of the International Institute on Alcoholism and Drug Addiction, Switzerland, came to South Africa in August for talks with the South African Minister of Social Welfare, Dr C. P. Mulder and for a series of seminars in Johannesburg. In the photograph Mr Tongue, left, meets with Dr Mulder in Pretoria.

Photo: CSIR, Pretoria
The CSIR's experimental autogyro, which has been under design, construction and development during the past eight years, flew successfully for the first time on November 30, 1972. The autogyro project was begun by the CSIR's Aeronautics Research Unit (ARU) eight years ago. One of the objectives was to establish the design principles of a short take-off and landing (STOL) machine which, it was believed, would have great potential for a wide range of useful applications if successfully developed. As far as is known, the CSIR autogyro is the only one of its size flying in the world at present with this simple rotor system. The experimental prototype was designed for a maximum speed of 160 km/h and a minimum cruising speed of 43 km/h.

Photo: Pretoria News
An international symposium on game capturing was held at the Onderstepoort Veterinary Research Institute in July. Delegates from a number of Southern African countries attended. In the photograph appears from left to right Dr E. Young, Chairman, Dr D. Phonoro of Lesotho, Mr B. Rasereko from Botswana and Dr H. Ebedes, secretary of the symposium.

Photo: S.A. Digest
Dr Jacob Seretlo, the first Black South African to receive his doctorate in Physics from the University of South Africa.

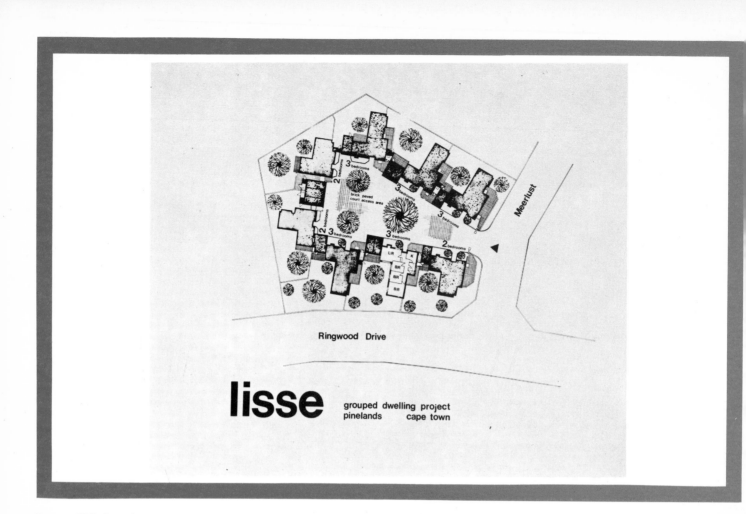

lisse grouped dwelling project
pinelands   cape town

Ringwood Drive

Meerlust

Photos: CSIR, Pretoria

1. This concept illustrates how the Sectional Titles Act will make possible in South Africa the ownership of a comfortable home within a high density housing scheme.

2. This high density housing project was designed to provide home owners with the privacy of a courtyard.

3. A view of the courtyard illustrates the neat arrangement and spacious atmosphere created in the design of this project.

In recent years cities in South Africa have been developing so rapidly that meeting the housing requirements of urban dwellers has become a major problem. The National Building Research Institute launched a long-term research investigation starting with an international symposium on high density housing in Johannesburg held during September 1972.

Projects are being planned in which balanced mixtures of high and low-rise buildings are to be grouped in independent village units, each with its own neighbourhood facilities. The psychological needs of the individual will be a basic consideration in the design of such schemes. The buildings will be set amid open parkland surrounded by gardens and provision will be made for facilities such as hospitals, libraries and theatres. NBRI researchers are continually improving the basic ideals of housing with the objective of creating a city in which even Aristotle would have been able to live happily.

4. The home owner in a high density housing project can still enjoy the sunshine in his private, if modest, garden.

Photo: S.A. Digest
Professor E. M. van Zinderen Bakker, Head of the University of the Orange Free State's Department of Botany and Mr P. A. le Roux, a member of the Weather Bureau, who received the South African Antarctic Association's Gold Medal. This was the first time the award has been made for work in the sub-Antarctic islands, mostly on Prince Edward, Gough and Marion Island.

Photo: Fuel Research Institute, Pretoria
Dr H. T. Sorgnit of the Fuel Research Institute of South Africa with the world's first fully smokeless stove designed as a do-it-yourself construction set. The new principle evolved obviates the emission of smoke by burning off all the volatile matter of ordinary bituminous coal in a unique refractory channel before it can reach the chimney as smoke.

Photo: Fuel Research Institute, Pretoria
Mr F. O. Heim of the Fuel Research Institute of South Africa with a Diesel engine converted to run virtually smokelessly on diesolene which is augmented at peak power demands by liquid petroleum gas, without any loss of power or any extra running costs. This dual fuel techinque eliminates the black clouds of smoke so often emitted by Diesel engines powered by diesolene only.

Photo: Daily News, Durban
A fracture in the Durban-Johannesburg oil pipeline in June created a first rate crisis. Post authorities at Durban harbour, Africa's biggest, feared a flash ignition as oil flowed into the Umbilo Canal. Vast amounts of chemicals were sprayed by tugs and even by handbucket, as seen in the photograph, to avert disaster.

Photo: Perskor
Striking British dockworkers interrupted their action in August to offload a cargo of 15 White rhinos from South Africa. Here Yashin Smart, daughter of a well known circus group, keeps an eye on the first rhino nosing his way out of the cage.

Photo: Natal Mercury

The little animal on the left is known as a Zeedonk. In December embarrassed officials at the Natal Institute of Immunology announced the birth of a Zeedonk foal to the Zebra mare in the picture. The father, a nondescript donkey, seen on the right, was not part of the immunology experiment.

Photo: Perskor

Dr P. G. du Plessis was awarded the 1972 Hertzog Prize for Drama for his work *Siener in the Suburbs,* also taking into account his drama *Die nag van Legio.* The prize is the most coveted award in Afrikaans literature and has been awarded only seven times since 1926.

Photo: Perskor

Professor Rob Antonissen died in Port Elizabeth on September 23. He was one of the best known literary critics in South Africa and, at the time of his death Head of the Department of Afrikaans and Netherlands at Rhodes University, Grahamstown. His death (at 53) was due to lung cancer.

Photo: SA Parks Board

An international conference at the World Wildlife Associations Fund in Switzerland named South Africa as the country where research in game ranching was the most highly developed. The Fund announced in November that it would conduct research in South Africa on the commercial production of meat and other game products from game ranching. The photograph shows Zebra at a drinking place in one of South Africa's many game reserves.

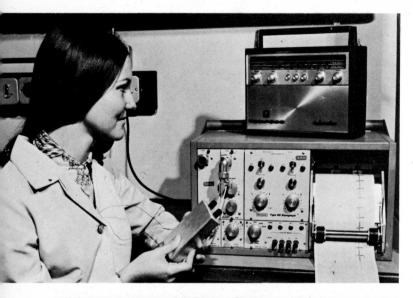

Photo: CSIR, Pretoria

A tiny radio telemetry system for monitoring the electrocardiogram of cardiac patients has been developed by the medical electronic research team of South Africa's Council for Scientific and Industrial Research. The battery powered system is pocket sized and transmits heart function data to a central monitor unit. This promises greater personal freedom to cardiac patients. Here a CSIR technician listens to her own heartbeat being received by a conventional transistor radio.

Photo: S.A. Digest

In July the first South African Nursing Association congress to be held in a Black homeland took place in Umtata, capital of the Transkei. One of the main speakers was Miss S. N. Sigcau, Transkeian Minister of Education.

Photo: Pretoria University

The first medical dictionary in the Afrikaans language was officially released at a function held at the Medical Faculty of the University of Pretoria in June. Here Professor E. M. Hamman, Principal of U.P., receives the first copy from Professor H. W. Snyman, right, Dean of the Faculty and compiler of the dictionary.

Photo: Nasionale Koerante, Cape Town

Sound is now listed as a pollution in South Africa. At the University of Cape Town a new Sound Research Institute was established in 1972. Here the head, Dr Adelbert Semmelink, operates apparatus used to analyse sounds. Dr Semmelink is currently working on a project for the use of sound in the even filtration of liquids.

Photo: The Star, Johannesburg

Professor P. V. Tobias (right) and Senator van der Spuy after the latter had unveiled a plaque on the Melville Koppies to inaugurate the Museums of Man and Science Fund on November 7. Professor Tobias is holding the fossilised skull of the Taungs woman, identified by Professor Raymond Dart as that of one of the earliest hominids, Australopithecus africanus. Speaking at the ceremony, the professor paid tribute to South African archeologists who have contributed to the knowledge of early man in Africa. The museums, he said, would draw scientists and scholars from all over the world and the knowledge so gained would enable man to survive in the strange, new world he is creating.

Photo: Perskorporasie van S.A.

Professor S. F. Oosthuizen — known to doctors throughout South Africa as the Republic's "Father of Radiology" — has been awarded the first gold Founders' Medal of the Radiological Society of South Africa. Professor Oosthuizen, who has been president of the SA Medical Council since 1951, is well known internationally.

The new gold medal is his third and one of the many top awards he has received during his career.

Photo: Pretoria University

Professor P. J. Kloppers, Director of the new Hans Snyckers Institute at Pretoria University. The Institute was founded to specialize in the study of diseases endemic to South Africa.

Photo: S.A. Parks Board

In September the Kruger National Park gained a further twelve rare black rhinos. These huge animals, transported over 1500 kilometres from Kariba, were donated by the Rhodesian National Parks Board. The picture (right) shows the first black rhino moments after its release in the quarantine camp near Skukuza. (Photo: National Parks Board). In the picture (far right) veterinarians of the National Parks Board are seen treating 16 Kruger Park Cheetahs for virulent skin diseases. The infected animals were 'put to sleep' with special drug darts and then bathed in medicinal chemicals. (Photo: Africamera). Many of the larger animals are rarely plagued with skin deseases partly owing to their fondness of regular mud baths. The glistening hides of the Kruger Park Buffalo (pictured below) are a clear sign of a recent 'dip' in some cosy mudhole.

Photo: Perskor

HUNUC, South Africa's first underwater laboratory — underwent its first preliminary tests at Salisbury Island in Durban Harbour. The steel habitat, weighing more than 24 tons, was launched in May by the Chief of the Navy, Vice-Admiral J. Johnson.

Photo: Volksblad, Bloemfontein

A scale model of Bloemfontein's new academic hospital and medical faculty which is currently being built.

Photo: Nasionale Koerante, Cape Town

Fledgling scientists en route to foreign shores. Four of the twelve winners of the Science Week competition organised by the Foundation for Education, Science and Technology. These gifted science pupils are here seen departing from Cape Town for a two-week science course in London. They are from left to right: Robert Gush, Martin Shapiro, Roy Maartens and (second from right) Addie Beyers.

Photo: The Argus, Cape Town

As though shielding his eyes from the sight of a pollution stricken environment, from which even the birds are fleeing, with pigeons in the foreground symbolizing nature's protest against environmental despoliation, the equestrian statue at Rhodes Memorial on the slopes of Devil's Peak, Cape Town, towers above the eastern suburbs of the Mother City. Fortunately, South Africa has already begun to marshal its resources to combat growing air and water pollution. The Secretary for Transport, Mr J. Driessen, announced in Pretoria on November 9, that a new law to punish ships polluting coastal waters would come into effect in 1973. The S.A. Iron and Steel Corporation (Iscor), announced on August 30, that in 10 years it would increase expenditure on anti-pollution measures by 20 per cent — to R120 million. The Minister of Planning, Mr J. Loots, said that his department was now a Department of the Environment in all but name. He urged provincial, state and local authorities to apply to the fullest existing anti-pollution laws and regulations. In September the Fuel Research Institute announced a unique breakthrough against smog with the development of the world's first fully smokeless stove.

7

Sport and recreation

Photos: Africamera
The Federation Cup, the top international tournament for women tennis, was held in South Africa for the first time. In the end the South African team of Pat Pretorius, Brenda Kirk and Greta Delport scored the Republic's first victory in this competition. The photographs show the visiting teams lined up for the official opening and the Minister of Sports and Recreation, Mr Frank Waring, welcoming the Japanese side. Other photographs show Pat Pretorius and Brenda Kirk (right) performing a victory dance after winning the decisive doubles match, and the Prime Minister, Mr B. J. Vorster, congratulating the winners.

Photo: Africamera
Five of the world's top jockeys participated in the annual International Jockeys' horse race at the Scottsville course in Natal. The photograph shows (from left) Takemi Kaga, Japan's champion jockey for eight years, Tony Murray (Ireland), Fernando Toro (America), Don Pierce (America) and Brian Andrews (New Zealand). They were joined by England's champion jockey, Willie Carson, and Australian Bill Camer.

Bob Hewitt (left) and Frew McMillan, one of the world's most successful men's doubles pairs ever, won the Wimbledon title for the second time. (Previously in 1967.) They dropped only one set during the tournament; in 1967 they did not lose a single set.

Photo: Africamera
Australia's John Newcombe, three times winner at Wimbledon, won the men's singles in the Castle Cup tennis tournament at Ellis Park, Johannesburg. The photograph shows the power and determination that brought Newcombe victory.

Photo: Hoofstad
The annual Orange Bowl tennis tournament at Miami Beach attracts the world's best junior players. South Africa enjoyed a very successful year in 1972, with Pretoria's Deon Joubert and Bernie Mitton winning the doubles title.

Photo: Africamera
Cliff Richey plays a flying back-hand volley on his way to becoming the first American since Earl Buchholz in 1960, to win the South African singles tennis title for men. Richey beat Spain's Manuel Orantes in the final.

Photo: Die Burger, Cape Town

A junior South African rugby football team, the Gazelles, toured the Argentine. They seemed set to return with an unbeaten record, but were beaten 18-16 in the second and final test. The photograph shows Travaglini (Argentine) kicking ahead when challenged by the South African captain, Jannie van Aswegen (with sweat band).

Photo: Perskor

In the final of South Africa's premier rugby football competition, Transvaal beat their neighbours, Eastern Transvaal, thereby winning the Currie Cup for the second year in succession. The photograph shows Transvaal scrum-half, Paul Bayvel, off and running, with opponents in hot pursuit. This was the first time in twenty years that Transvaal become sole holder of the coveted trophy.

Photo: Africamera

England won the only test of a seven-match short rugby tour of South Africa when they beat the Springboks 18-9 at Johannesburg's Ellis Park stadium. The photograph shows South African wing Syd Nomis being firmly tackled, ball and all.

Photo: The Star, Johannesburg
More than a hunderd professional golfers from nine countries participated in the R25 000 multi-national Louis Luyt PGA golf tournament at the Wanderers, Johannesburg. Here Moses Magoro (South Africa) and Canadian Rob Dearden have a chat while waiting for their turn to tee off.

Photo: Africamera, Johannesburg

South Africa's first multi-national athletics delegation seen leaving from Jan Smuts Airport, Johannesburg, on a goodwill tour which took them to Greece, Turkey, Italy, Switzerland, Belgium, France, England, Denmark, Sweden, Norway and Finland. One of the purposes of the tour was to contact top athletes with a view to inviting them to compete in the multi-national South African Games to be held in Pretoria in April 1973. Checking their tickets are Mr Gert Potgieter, former world record holder for the 440 yards, Mr Edward Sethsedi, an official of the South African African Athletics Organisation, and Mr Gert le Roux (right), secretary of the South African Amateur Athletics Union.

Photo: The Star

The South African Football Association's "Top Level" committee, appointed to further the aims of non-white football in the Republic, met in Johannesburg for discussions. Among the subjects was the pending congress of the international football federation, FIFA. The committee included representatives from the white South African Football Association, the South African Indian Football Association, the South African Coloured Football Association, and the South African Bantu Football Association.

Photo: Perskorporasie van S.A.

South Africa's Federation Cup tennis team was elected after trials in which four leading black players also participated. Pat Pretorius (left) and Brenda Kirk (right) were chosen at the conclusion of the trials and went on to win the world's major women's team competition.

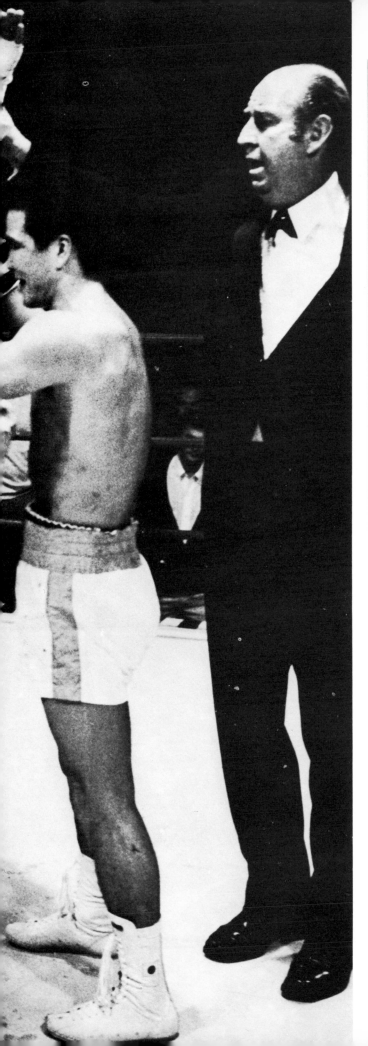

Photo: Pretoria News, Pretoria
Among the many sports teams to visit the Republic in 1972 was the all-American senior amateur wrestling team. The photograph shows Johan van Zyl of the South African Defence Force lifting American Mike Jones clear off the mat on his way to victory in the 60 kg match. The visitors, however, went on to win the tournament 7-3.

Photo: Hoofstad
At the ninth Zauli memorial international athletics meeting in Rome, South African Fanie van Zijl won the 1 500 metres comfortably, beating world mile record-holder Jim Ryun.
Van Zijl clocked 3 min 39,7 seconds, beating second-placed McDonald (Canada) and third-placed Ryun by more than four seconds.

Photo: Perskor
Moment of triumph: South African lightweight champion, Andries Steyn, receiving the congratulations of opponent Kuniaki Shibata after he had scored a convincing points victory over the former world featherweight champion from Japan.

99

Photo: Africamera
Golfer Gary Player (left) won the Sportsman of the Year trophy for the sixth time. In recognition of this feat, he was also acclaimed Sportsman of the Decade. Among Player's achievements in 1972 were victories in the United States PGA championship — the second time he has won this event — and the Piccadilly World Series in Britain.

Photo: Africamera
The year saw South Africa's first open international squash circuit. The four-tournament circuit drew world stars like Australia's Geoff Hunt, ranked first in the world, and Sharif Khan (left) of Pakistan.

Photo: The Argus, Cape Town
Dicky Broberg displays the Helms Trophy Award for the Continent of Africa, presented to him by the Prime Minister, Mr B. J. Vorster, in the Houses of Parliament, Cape Town. Broberg received the trophy for achieving the fastest 800 metres time since the 1968 Olympics — it was also the best time achieved by a runner anywhere in the world in 1971.

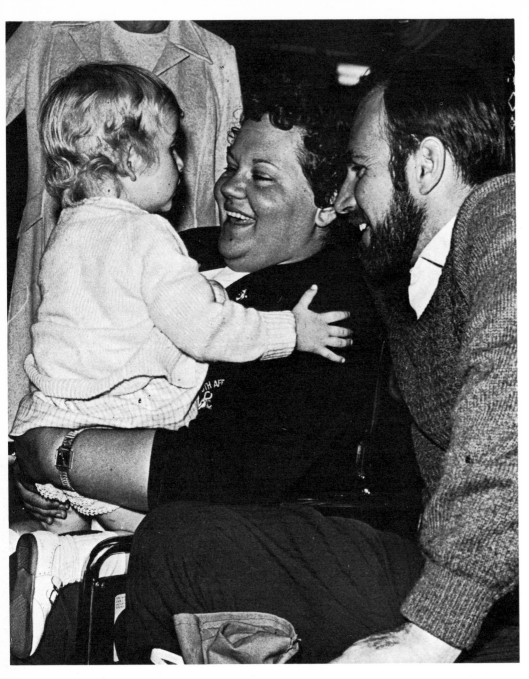

Photo: Perskor
The South African paraplegic team won 48 medals to gain fourth place at the Para-Olympics held at Heidelberg, West Germany. The photograph shows silver medalist Mrs Eteria Wolvaardt being welcomed by her daughter and husband on the team's return to South Africa.

8

The arts
and entertainment

Photo: Africamera
The Israeli ensemble, Hatzabarim, at Jan Smuts Airport before
flying to Durban for the first leg of their South African tour.
The group, comprising 25 girls and boys, excells in jazz based on
Hebrew and Arabic music.

Photo: Pretoria University

The Drama Department of the University of Pretoria achieved a notable success with its presentation of Electra. Main reason for the success was the magnificent performance of Miss Aleka Katseli, leading actress of the Greek National Theatre (in the role of Clytemnestra). Miss Katseli was specially invited by the Drama Department to perform in Neels Hansen's production of the famous Greek tragedy.

Photo: Perskor

Jerry Lewis, one of the world's most popular comedians visited South Africa on a two-week tour in October. In the picture he is seen presenting the coveted Sarie award to a popular South African light vocalist, Alan Garrity.

LAUSANNE 72

Photo: Africamera

Photo: Samuel Kok

During the fourth International Festival of Youth Orchestras in the Palais de Beaulieu in Lausanne, Switzerland, the 70-member Junior Orchestra of the South African Broadcasting Corporation, with conductor Walter Mony, acquitted itself with distinction. The picture (above) was taken during a performance by these talented musicians in the Palais. One of these youngsters, 16-year old Peter Rohner (pictured right), earned a coveted one-year-scholarship to study the violin under Professor Max Rostal at Berne. Julienne Fitchett, (pictured far right) was elected as assistant conductor of the International Orchestra for Ballet.

Photo: Perskor

Teresa Berganza, the celebrated Spanish coloratura mezzo-soprano, made a brief recital tour through South Africa in November. The renowned opera star, seen here being interviewed by the press, was accompanied by her husband, Felix Lavilla, an accomplished musician in his own right.

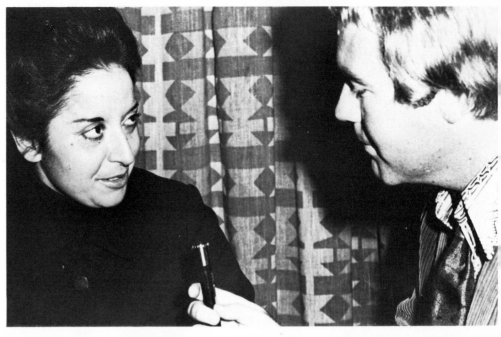

Photo: Perskor

Six of the guest dancers who performed traditional dances in Johannesburg. Representing nine nationalities, these girls visited the Republic at the invitation of the Transvaal Committee for Folksong and Folk Dancing.

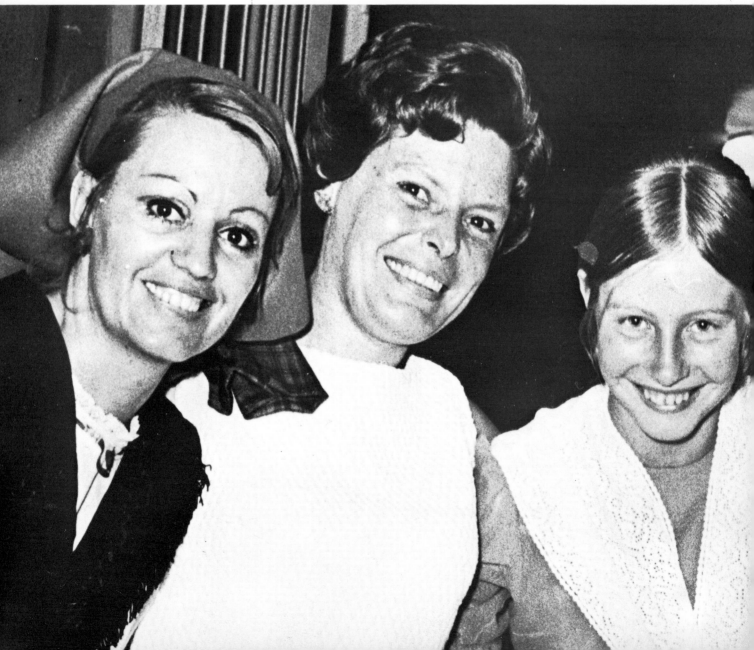

os: Perskor

st Jankowski's visit to the Republic in October proved to be one of the show business
lights of the year. The world famous German jazz pianist (picture right), together with
estra and choir, has topped the German TV popularity pools for the past four years. An added
ction of no small renown, was Rolf Kuhn (pictured above), acknowledged by many critics as
world's top jazz clarinetist.

Photo: The Star, Johannesburg
Radiating charm, beauty and personality, Yvette Mimieux, the famous Hollywood star, arrived in Johannesburg in July to attend the Metro Goldwyn Mayer Convention in Johannesburg. Another celebrated guest was Robert Mitchum, famous American film personality. The picture (above) shows the famous star and his wife, Dorothy, being engulfed by a mass of fans.

Photo: Africamera
Kenichi Nishida, the first Japanese painter to exhibit in the Trias gallery in Johannesburg's Carlton Centre. The exhibition was opened by Mr Kenichir Nishizawa, the Japanese Consul General in South Africa.

Photo: Pact
Pierre Fournier, the internationally celebrated French cellist, was the soloist with the SABC National Orchestra at the opening of the symphony season in Johannesburg.

Photo: Africamera

The touring Melos String Quartet found great favour with South African audiences. This famous German group do about 120 concerts a year devoting itself entirely to chamber music.

Photo: The Star, Johannesburg

Three of the four violin-playing sons of Mr and Mrs Nat Zwane of Durban passed their first practical examination with England's famous Trinity College of Music — an unusual distinction by any standard. The boys are, from left to right: Trevor (10), who has not passed yet, Darryl (10, and Trevor's twin), Bertrand (12) and Ashmore (13).

113

Photo: The Star, Johannesburg
This antique Dresden porcelain urn, one of a set called Fire and Water, was one of the pieces from a valuable collection auctioned in Johannesburg during August. The collection belonged to the late Mr I. Goodlesser, a well-known collector and student of antiques.

Photo: PACT
Joyce Barker, the celebrated South African soprano, made her Covent Garden debut in April in the star soprano role of Verdi's Don Carlos. She subsequently sang the leading role in Macbeth at Glyndelbourne in June and July. A special version of the Verdi opera was produced by Southern Television for general release. The picture shows Joyce Barker, in the leading role of Turandot.

Photo: Africamera
Trophy for a winner. South African sculptress Rhona Stern and the striking bronze trophy she created for the Holiday Inns Handicap, the Republic's richest horse race, involving a massive R80 000 stake.

Veruschka, the world's highest paid model, interrupted her globe-trotting to pay a short visit to Johannesburg.

Photos: PACT

When the orchestra of the Performing Arts Council of the Transvaal (PACT) started its third symphony season in November, it was the very first time that it had a woman as leader of the orchestra. This distinction was earned by Annie Kossman, the well-known South African violinist, who lead the PACT Orchestra at five concerts. PACT also employed the services of Louis Fremaux, resident conductor of the Birmingham Symphony Orchestra (picture left). He was guest conductor for a series of seven concerts with PACT's Symphony Orchestra in June.

Photo: Africamera

Mr Harry Mekéle and Mrs. Grace Senne are clearly delighted with the star treatment they receive at the Johannesburg premiere of the film "Liefde vir Lelik", in which they both appear.

117

Photo: Natal Mercury
George Msimang, who returned to Durban after a year's study in Rome on a scholarship at the Academia de Belle Arti. The picture shows the artist with one of his drawings, entitled Musicians, exhibited in Durban.

Photo: Die Volksblad, Bloemfontein
Actress Trudy Taljaard and director Pieter Fourie discuss the surrealistic decor for the Performing Arts Council of the Free State's Afrikaans production of Friedrich Dürrenmatt's *Die Ehe des Herrn Mississippi,* under the title: *Olympia en Haar Vryers* (Olympia and her suitors). Danish-born Raymond Schoop designed the decor.

Photo: Africamera
Victor Borge, famous Danish musician and comedian arrived in South Africa in July for a five week concert tour.

Photo: Nasionale Koerante
Stefans Grové, the internationally known South African composer, returned to the Republic after a ten year stay in the U.S.A. He is seen here with his wife Rashi and two sons, Tristan (in front) and Claude-Francois.

Photo: Africamera
Six members of the world famous German dancing team, the Opitz Formation, introduce themselves to South Africa. The groups gave exhibition performances in Johannesburg, Durban and Port Elizabeth. From the left: Peter and Elfie Matthiesen, Rainer and Ceke Schönau and Nico Lembke and Petra Ellerbrook.

Photo: Napac

BASIL HOSKINS, famous British star (now in the musical "Applause" opposite Lauren Bacall in London's West End), came to South Africa for the first time last year to star in the musical "Don't Listen Ladies!" from the book and lyrics by Guy Bolton and Jill Fenson and music by the South African-born composer George de Jongh. The production was not without drama when the leading lady, Deborah Witkin, was taken seriously ill and had to be replaced at two days notice by Jill Fenson, who is seen here with Mr Hoskins in the final moments of the musical.

Photo: Napac

Some of the enchanting characters created by A. A. Milne in his fantasy "Winnie-the-Pooh" were brought to life by NAPAC in the South African premiere of a new musical adaptation of the book. In the picture are, from left to right, Bill Smale as Piglet; Ian Hamilton as Pooh; James Irwin as Eeyore; Deniece Grobler as Kanga with Trevor Dodd (in the foreground) as Tiger and David Horner (in the background) as Owl. "Winnie-the-Pooh" was produced by Geoffrey Sutherland and the show ran through the Christmas New York period from 1971 to 1972.

121

JANET COSTER, internationally acclaimed singer, came to Durban in May to sing the title role in "Carmen" opposite Gé Korsten — in a production directed by James Conrad and designed by Christina Oosthuizen and Tom Owen.

EMRYS JONES (left), the famous British star who made an enormous impact in Durban playing the role of the younger Winston Churchill in Guy Bolton's new play "A Man and His Wife" — a love story based on the life of Churchill and his beloved 'Clemmie'. In this picture with Mr Jones are Barbara Kinghorn as 'Clemmie' and David Exley as their friend, Archie. The play was later bought by a commercial management and taken to Johannesburg where a successful run was interrupted by the sudden and tragic death of Mr Jones.

Photo: Napac

At the end of 1972 another children's production — "The Marvellous Story of Puss in Boots" by the British playwright Nicholas Stuart Gray, was presented for the delight of Durban and Natal audiences — for "Puss in Boots" was the first of the spectacular Christman productions which NAPAC was able to take to the country towns. In this scene Puss (right), played by Mary Harrison, tries to restrain the wicked orge, played by James Irwin, from attacking Gerard and Dandy, Mervyn Goodman and Lynette Brown.

123

Willem de la Querra as Giepie, the peddler, in Capac's presentation of "Die Towerboek van Kammalielieland". A highlight of Capac's Children's Theatre, this comedy attracted enthusiastic audiences throughout the Western and Eastern Cape.

Phyllis Spira, Capab Ballet's principal dancer, rehearses her lead role in Fiesta Manchega, one of three Spanish ballets performed at the Nico Malan Opera House in December.

Cobus Rossouw (centre) won the Honorary Award for Acting of the Suid-Afrikaanse Akademie vir Wetenskap en Kuns. The award is South Africa's highest in this field. The 39-year-old actor is flanked by Professor F. C. L. Bosman (left) and Prof. H. L. de Waal of the Akademie.

Photos: PACT

The Performing Arts Council of the Transvaal (PACT) had a busy year and, judged from audience reaction, a highly successful one. Pictured are several scenes from some of its top presentations.

The picture (left) is a scene from the Cuban writer Leehardo Manet's macabre comedy *"The Nuns"*, presented in Johannesburg. Pictured (right) is a scene from *"Alice's Adventures Underground"*, with David van der Merwe (King of Hearts), Nill Aamand (White Hare), Nan Gray (Alice) and Ina Cornell (Queen of Hearts).

The production staged in Johannesburg was adapted by Nigel Vermaas from Lewis Carroll's "Alice's Adventures in Wonderland" and "Alice Through the Looking Glass".

Photos: PACT

Pictured (above) are George Ballot as Mortimer and Marius Weyers as Leicester in Truida Louw's production of Schiller's *"Maria Stuart"*. The picture (left) depicts a scene from *"Die Seemeeu",* Afrikaans translation of Chekov's *"The Seagull"*, with Sandra Prinsloo as Nina Zarjetsjnaia and Don Lampbrecht as Kostja Trepliow (directed by Robert Mohr).

Photos: Pact
Some more scenes from Pact presentations. Sir Robert Helpmann (left) and Sir Frederick Ashton as the step-sisters in the ballet "Cinderella" presented by Pact Ballet in Johannesburg. (top right) Natalia Makarova — famous Russian ballerina, and Ivan Nagy, in Giselle. (centre) A scene from Donizetti's Don Pasquale, with Rita Roberts as Narina and George Kok as Ernesto.

9

People, places and events

Photo: Africamera

Two Durban girls, Cynthia Shenge (right) and Stephanie Reinecke, Miss Africa South and Miss South Africa, respectively, represented the Republic at the Miss World competition in London. Here both girls display dresses with an African motif.

Photo: The Star, Johannesburg

The King of the Zulu nation, Paramount Chief Goodwill Zwelithini (centre), wearing his leopard regalice, about to lead Zulu dancers in traditional regimental dancing at the Western Deep Levels Gold Mine, near Johannesburg. King Zwelithini was on a goodwill visit to see and meet Zulus employed on the Witwatersrand, the gold mining region stretching to the east and to the west of Johannesburg.

Photo: Africamera
The establishment of a Republic of South Africa has been the great ideal of Mr J. G. Strijdom, Prime Minister of South Africa from 1954 to 1958, although he did not live to see this idea fulfilled. During a Republic Day ceremony in Pretoria the former leader's widow unveiled the impressive Strijdom Monument. The monument consists of a large white dome, sheltering a bronze bust of South Africa's fifth Prime Minister, and, in the foreground, a pillar washed by a fountain and surmounted by a sculptured group of running horses. Mrs Strijdom and sculptor Coert Steynberg stand below the bust of the former leader.

Photo: Natal Daily News
Among the many colourful visitors to South Africa in 1972 were the Venerable Lama Anagarika Govinda, head of the Arya Maitreya Mandala order of Tibet, and his wife, Li Gotami.

Photo: S.A. Digest

The "father" of the South African Air Force and leader of the country's armed forces throughout World War Two, General Sir Pierre van Ryneveld, died at Pretoria at the age of 81. In 1920 he and the late Sir Quintin Brand were knighted when they made history as the first men to fly from Britain to South Africa. The flight took 45 days. The photograph shows Sir Pierre (right) at his last public appearance, celebrating the golden jubilee of the South African Air Force. He is shown chatting to Lt.-Gen. J. P. Verster, Air Force Chief (left).

Photo: Africamera, Johannesburg

Aleka Katseli, leading actress of the National Theatre of Greece, visited the Republic to conduct a course of lectures for the drama faculty of the University of Pretoria. She also appeared on stages in various parts of the country to perform some of the great classical roles in her repertoire. She has for many years been the permanent "priestess" at the ceremony of lighting the Olympic Torch to be carried to the Olympic Games. Here she is greeted by her friend and leading South African theatre producer, Taubie Kushlick (with hat), on her arrival in Johannesburg.

Photo: Perskor

South African Airways' chief pilot, Captain Salmon "Pi" Pienaar, welcomed by his wife at the completion of his final flight as pilot. Captain Pienaar commenced his distinguished flying career in 1938. Because of his position, "Pi" Pienaar has qualified to fly all the aircraft of the S.A.A., the only officer to do so. After a flying career of almost 35 years, and more than 18 000 flying hours, Captain Pienaar takes over the job of Director of Aviation, one of the four top posts in South African Airways.

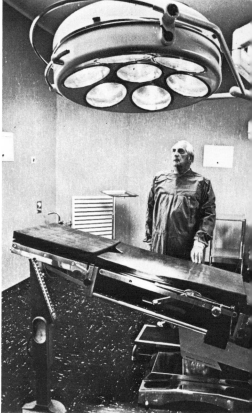

Photos: Pretoria News

In standard and scope South Africa's medical services for all its different population groups are far in advance of the rest of Africa. The biggest hospital in Africa — and one of the biggest specialist hospitals in the world — is the Baragwanath Hospital for black people near Johannesburg, where some 24 000 operations are performed and over 700 000 out-patients treated annually. In 1972 the first wards opened at Kalafong, Pretoria's new 850-bed hospital for black people erected at a cost of R5-million. The hospital has 11 operating theatres, an elaborate intensive-care unit, a disaster centre and one of the best radiology units in the country. Of the 175 doctor's posts, 71 are for specialists. A resident patient with an income of less than R500 p.a. pays less than one American dollar or less than 3 Swiss francs or less than 25 British New Pence — this includes operations and is irrespective of the duration of the time spent in the hospital. The photographs show the partly completed hospital and one of the operating theatres.

Photo: Pretoria News

Sergeant J. W. Fouché was awarded the South African Police Star for Merit for saving the lives of 104 people trapped by raging floods in the Eastern Cape Province in August 1971. During one incident he jumped on to a building's roof and lifted 31 Coloured men, women and children shoulder high on to a helicopter — the people did not understand how to use the helicopter's cable lift, or were too weak to hoist themselves up.

Photo: Africamera

Dr Barry Cohen became the first South African to be elected an International Director of Lions International. Dr Cohen was elected at the organisation's annual convention in Mexico City. The movement, whose object is service to the community, has a world membership of nearly a million and representatives from 147 countries or areas attended the five-day convention. The photograph shows Dr and Mrs Cohen on their arrival in South Africa from Mexico. Dr Cohen will serve for two years on the 24 man executive as representative of Africa and South East Asia.

Photo: S.A. Digest

South Africa's confidence in gold's future was reflected by the official opening of a new gold mine, the East Driefontein mine. Performing the opening, Mr A. Louw, chairman of the Goldfields of South Africa group, said that his group's decisions were not based on a gold price related to either monetary or speculative considerations, but on studies of supply and demand, and these studies showed a steadily increasing shortfall between industrial demand and supply. The photograph shows gold being poured at a South African gold mine.

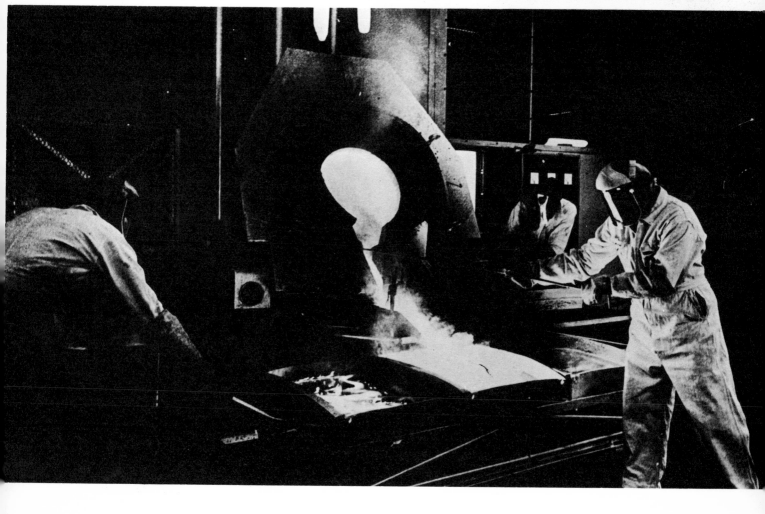

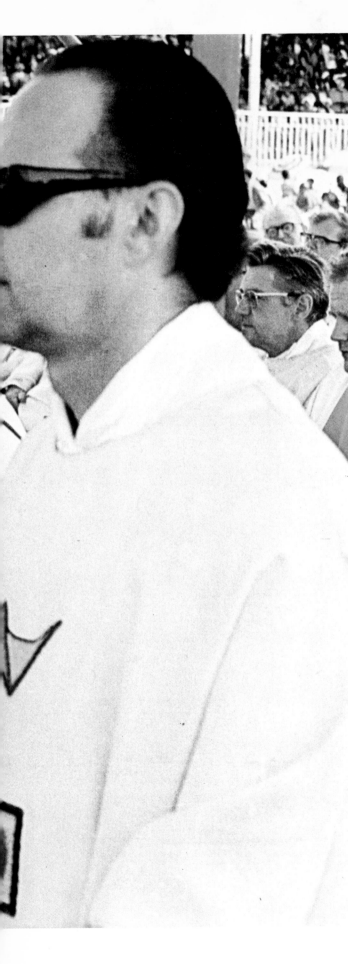

Photo: Nasionale Koerante, Cape Town

A pupil of Cape Town's Greek school, in traditional Greek dress, and Archbishop Pavlos of the Cape of Good Hope (right) welcomed Nicolas VI, Patriarch of Alexandria and the whole of Africa, at the beginning of his South African visit. This was the Patriarch's second visit, the first being in September 1969, a year after he had become head of the church. His church has approximately 250 000 members in Africa, of whom about 50 000 reside in South Africa.

Photo: Nasionale Koerante, Cape Town

American singer Eartha Kitt (centre) and actress Joan Fontaine (right) were among the guests at a reception held in Cape Town in honour of visiting British ballerina, Dame Margot Fonteyn. Dame Margot (left) is obviously enjoying the story Eartha Kitt is telling.

Photo: Africamera

Johannesburg's first black Roman Catholic bishop, Bishop Peter Buthelezi (red cap, centre), being consecrated at Milner Park, Johannesburg.

141

Photo: Nasionale Koerante, Cape Town
One of the world's leading cantors, Moshe Stern, arriving at Cape Town for a singing tour of the Republic. He wife, Zipora, seems to be equally pleased with the prospect of their visit. In 1958 Stern was appointed chief cantor of the "Hechal Shlomo", one of Israel's most prominent synagogues, and since 1968 he has been chief cantor of New York's Beth-El temple.

Photo: Cape Argus
Dr P. A. Helley, ichthyologist at the South African Museum, seems quite pleased with what he sees. He is looking at the world record long-fin tunney boated by Mr Brain Cohen of Fish Hoek, near Cape Town. The fish weighted 31,7 kg, reportedly bettering the world record by 0,45 kg.

Photo: The Argus, Cape Town
Miss Dorothy Fisher, South Africa's longest surviving heart transplant patient, celebrated the third anniversary of her life with a new heart. Prof. Chris Barnard told her that he was very pleased with her condition. Miss Fisher said she felt first-class and added that she could eat and drink anything except fatty foods and that she was not subject to any dieting routine.

Photos: The Star, Johannesburg
Die Burger, Cape Town

In terms of tonnage involved, the world's biggest collision at sea was the 100 000-ton Greek-owned tanker *Texanita* explode and sink within minutes after colliding with the 95 000-ton Liberian tanker *Oswego Guardian* off the southern Cape coast. A total of 26 crewmen lost their lives. The damaged Liberian tanker (photo) limped to Cape Town with ruptured forepeak tanks and fire-blackened bows.

Photos: Rapport, Johannesburg
Die Burger, Cape Town

A number of student-police confrontations took place during June when groups of students protested against Government policy. In Cape Town and Johannesburg police batoncharged the demonstrators. The photographs show a student displaying his own brand of demonstration, and police dispersing students from the steps of St. George's Cathedral in Cape Town.

Photo: Perskor

The death occurred of Khotso Sethuntsa, the legendary Xhosa millionaire herbalist and property speculator who lived in a palatial mansion in the Transkei Territory. Two years previously, he celebrated his 87th birthday by taking his 24th wife. He has more than 200 children. His parents worked for President Paul Kruger, the famous Transvaal Boer president. The photograph shows Khotso and one of his sons.

144

Photo: Africamera
Macaki Ndzondzwana, of the East Daggafontein Goldmine, rescued another miner as blasting charges exploded round him at the mine. This earned Macaki the South African Chamber of Mines' Bronze Medal, also known as the "Miner's VC". Here he displays his awards, which included a gold watch and a cheque for R200.

Photo: The Star
Israeli and Bantu accents mingled when two black Johannesburg models, Dorcas Musi (second from left) and Felicia Buthelezi (second from right), met three visiting Israeli models, Hava Levy, Tami Levenstein and Ludmills Kuperman. The Israeli girls visited the Republic to model the latest Israeli fashions.

Photo: The Star
At the age of 96 Justus Chiroa flew home to Malawi "to die among my own people". For more than half a century Justus has worked for the Swart family of Brakpan, east of Johannesburg. Michael Swart (21 months), representing the fourth generation members of the Swart family Justus has known, saw the old man off on his last journey. A ground hostess guided Justus through formalities and on to the plane at Jan Smuts Airport, while in Malawi a social worker met him and put him on a train to Chintache, 650 kilometres away.

Photo: Richard Wege
Aerial view of an "instant housing" project for Coloured people at Bethelsdorp, Port Elizabeth. More than two thousand houses, varying from two to four bedrooms and including eleven different designs, were built at a rate of twenty per week. The precast concrete wall panels used provide as good sound, heat and moisture insulations as a concrete cavity wall 30 cm (11 inches) thick.

145

10

Statistical data

	1960	1970	1971
POPULATION (Millions)			
Total	16,0	21,4	22,0
Whites	3,1	3,8	3,9
Coloureds	1,5	2,0	2,1
Asians	0,5	0,6	0,6
Bantu Nations	10,9	15,0	15,4
MIGRATION (1 000)			
Immigrants	9,8	41,5	35,8
Emigrants	12,6	9,2	8,3
EMPLOYMENT (all races)			
Total (1 000)	1 635	2 455	2 522,0
Mining (1 000)	593	657	648,0
Private Manufacturing (1 000)	658	1 164	1 203,0
Construction (1 000)	126	356	384,0
Transport and Communications (1 000)	258	278*	287,0*
SALARIES AND WAGES			
Total (R million)	1 142,3	3 024,5*	3 385,9*
Mining	226,1	399,1	416,0
Manufacturing	577,7	1 609,2	1 820,3
Construction	74,5	436,6	501,8*
Transport and Communications	264,0	579,6*	647,8
UNEMPLOYMENT (1 000)			
Registered Unemployed (excl. Bantu)	25,7	8,5	8,6
CONSTRUCTION			
Building Plans approved (R million)	192,8	813,0	850,0
FOREIGN TRADE			
Imports (R million)	1 124	2 578	2 884,0
Exports (excl. gold) (R million)	881	1 420	1 531,0
GOLD SALES			
(R million)	536,0	830,3	892,8
TRANSPORT			
Railway Income (R million)	401,4	889,0	670,6
New Motor Vehicles registered (1 000)	118,0	250,8	267,2

*Estimated

GEOGRAPHICAL DISTRIBUTION OF WHITES, COLOUREDS, ASIANS AND BANTU IN WHITE AREAS AND BANTU HOMELANDS

YEAR	AREA	WHITES	%	COLRDS.	%	ASIANS	%	BANTU	%	TOTAL	%
1960*[2]	Total (R.S.A.)*[1]	3 088 492	100,0	1 509 258	100,0	477 125	100,0	10 927 922	100,0	16 002 797	100,0
	White Areas	3 064 555	98,07	1 494 113	98,98	470 619	98,63	6 819 968	62,40	11 849 255	73,93
	Bantu Homelands	23 937	0,87	15 145	1,00	6 506	1,36	4 107 954	37,58	4 153 542	25,91
1970*[2]	Total (R.S.A.)*[1]	3 750 716	100,0	2 018 533	100,0	620 422	100,0	15 057 559	100,0	21 447 230	100,0
	White Areas	3 729 959	99,44	2 005 390	99,34	616 981	99,44	8 059 325	53,51	14 411 655	67,01
	Bantu Homelands	20 757	0,55	13 143	0,65	3 441	0,55	6 998 234	46,46	7 035 575	32,72

*1 R.S.A. = Republic of South Africa
*2 Press Statement by Minister of Statistics, Republic of South Africa.

RACIAL DISTRIBUTION OF THE SOUTH AFRICAN POPULATION IN TOTAL FIGURES AND AS A PERCENTAGE OF THE TOTAL POPULATION

YEAR	WHITES	COLOUREDS	ASIANS	BANTU	TOTAL
1904[1]	1 117 234 (21,6)	444 991 (8,6)	122 311 (2,4)	3 490 291 (67,4)	2 174 827 (100,00)
1970[2]	3 750 716 (17,5)	2 018 533 (9,4)	620 422 (2,9)	15 057 559 (70,2)	21 447 230 (100,00)
2000[3]	7 033 000 (16,7)	5 831 000 (13,9)	1 159 000 (2,8)	27 949 000 (66,6)	41 972 000 (100,00)

[1] Republic of South Africa, Department of Statistics: Union Statistics for Fifty Years
[2] Press Statement by Minister of Statistics, Republic of South Africa
[3] Estimate of the Department of Statistics

HOME LANGUAGE OF THE SOUTH AFRICAN POPULATION*

POPULATION UNIT	HOME LANGUAGE	%	POPULATION UNIT	HOME LANGUAGE	%
WHITE NATION	Afrikaans	58,0	ASIAN COMMUNITY	Afrikaans	1,8
	English	37,1		English	14,4
	Afrikaans & English	1,6		Tamil	29,7
	Dutch	0,7		Gujarati	11,3
	German	1,0		Hindu	26,4
	Yiddish	0,2		Telegu	7,2
	Greek	0,3		Urdu	7,5
	Italian	0,4		Other Indian	0,4
	Portuguese	0,3		Chinese	1,0
	Other	0,4		Other	0,4
	Total	100,0		Total	100,0
COLOURED COMMUNITY	Afrikaans	88,6	BANTU PEOPLES	Xhosa	28,0
	English	10,1		Zulu	26,2
	Afrikaans & English	1,0		South Sotho	11,8
	Other	0,3		Tswana	10,5
	Total	100,0		Sepedi	8,8
				Shangaan	4,6
				Swazi	3,1
				Ndebele	2,7
				Venda	2,2
				Other	2,1
				Total	100,0

*Republic of South Africa, Department of Statistics: South African Statistics, 1968.

ECONOMICALLY ACTIVE POPULATION*

INDUSTRY GROUP	WHITES Percentage	COLOUREDS Percentage	ASIANS Percentage	BANTU Percentage
Agriculture	2,66	5,90	1,08	13,30
Mining	1,68	0,37	0,10	4,20
Manufacturing	7,51	8,36	10,26	3,40
Electricity	0,38	0,15	0,03	0,21
Construction	2,57	3,80	1,56	1,70
Commerce	7,33	3,84	8,24	2,09
Transport	4,39	1,36	1,22	0,92
Financing	3,91	0,34	0,46	0,23
Services	8,73	7,97	3,76	7,07
Unspecified	0,90	2,13	1,97	2,20
Unemployed	0,12	0,59	0,44	1,20
Total economically active	40,18	34,81	29,12	36,52

*Preliminary figures 1970 Population Census.

BANTU HOMELANDS IN SOUTH AFRICA

OFFICIAL NAME OF EACH HOMELAND AND ITS PEOPLE	CAPITAL	TERRITORY IN HECTARE	1970 POPULATION ('000)	CONSTITUTIONAL DEVELOPMENT LEGIS-LATIVE ASSEMBLY	SELF-GOVERN-MENT
				(YEARS IN WHICH STATUS WAS ATTAINED)	
1. Transkei (Xhosa)	Umtata	3 672 212	3 006	1963	1963
2. Ciskei (Xhosa)	Zwelitsha	918 547	924	1971	1972
3. KwaZulu (Zulu)	Nongoma[1]	3 144 421	4 026	1972	—
4. Lebowa (North Sotho)	Sheshego	2 214 086	2 019[3]	1971	1972
5. Venda (Vhavenda)	Sibasa	604 355	358	1971	1973
6. Gazankulu (Shangaan/Tsonga)	Giyani	667 292	737	1971	1973
7. Bophuthatswana (Tswana)	Mafeking[2]	3 754 018	1 719	1971	1972
8. Qwaqwa (South Sotho)	Qwaqua	45 742	1 452	1972	—
9. Swazi Territory (Swazi)	Nyamasane	211 807	499	—	—

[1] Capital to be transferred to Ulundi

[2] Capital to be transferred to Heystekrand

[3] De Jure population includes about 415 000 Ndebele-speaking people

SOURCE: Africa Institute, Pretoria.

1 hectare = 2,471 acres
100 hectare = 1 sq km = 0,386 sq miles

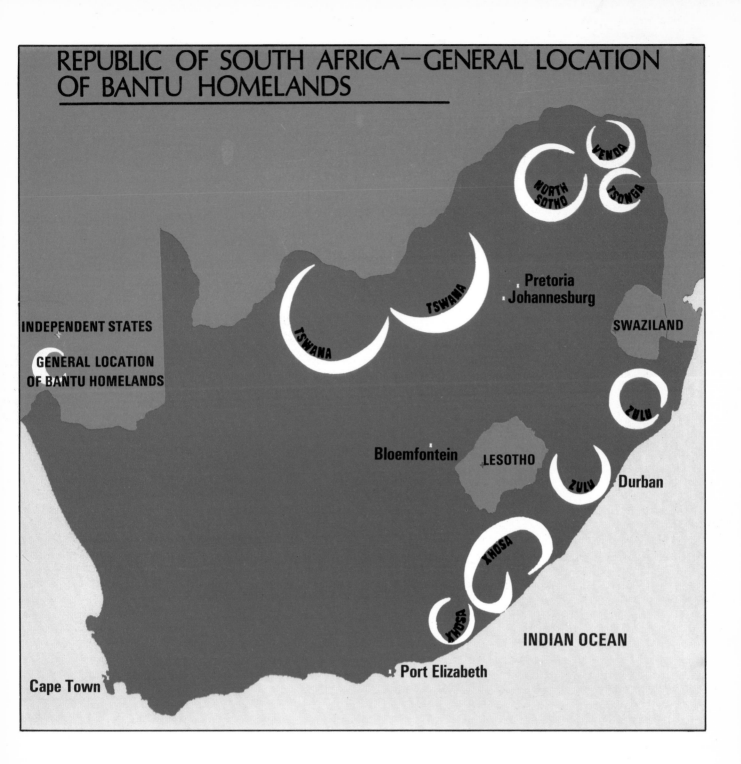

REPUBLIC OF SOUTH AFRICA—GENERAL LOCATION OF BANTU HOMELANDS

INDEPENDENT STATES

GENERAL LOCATION OF BANTU HOMELANDS

NORTH SOTHO

VENDA

TSONGA

TSWANA

TSWANA

Pretoria

Johannesburg

SWAZILAND

ZULU

Bloemfontein

LESOTHO

ZULU

Durban

XHOSA

XHOSA

INDIAN OCEAN

Port Elizabeth

Cape Town

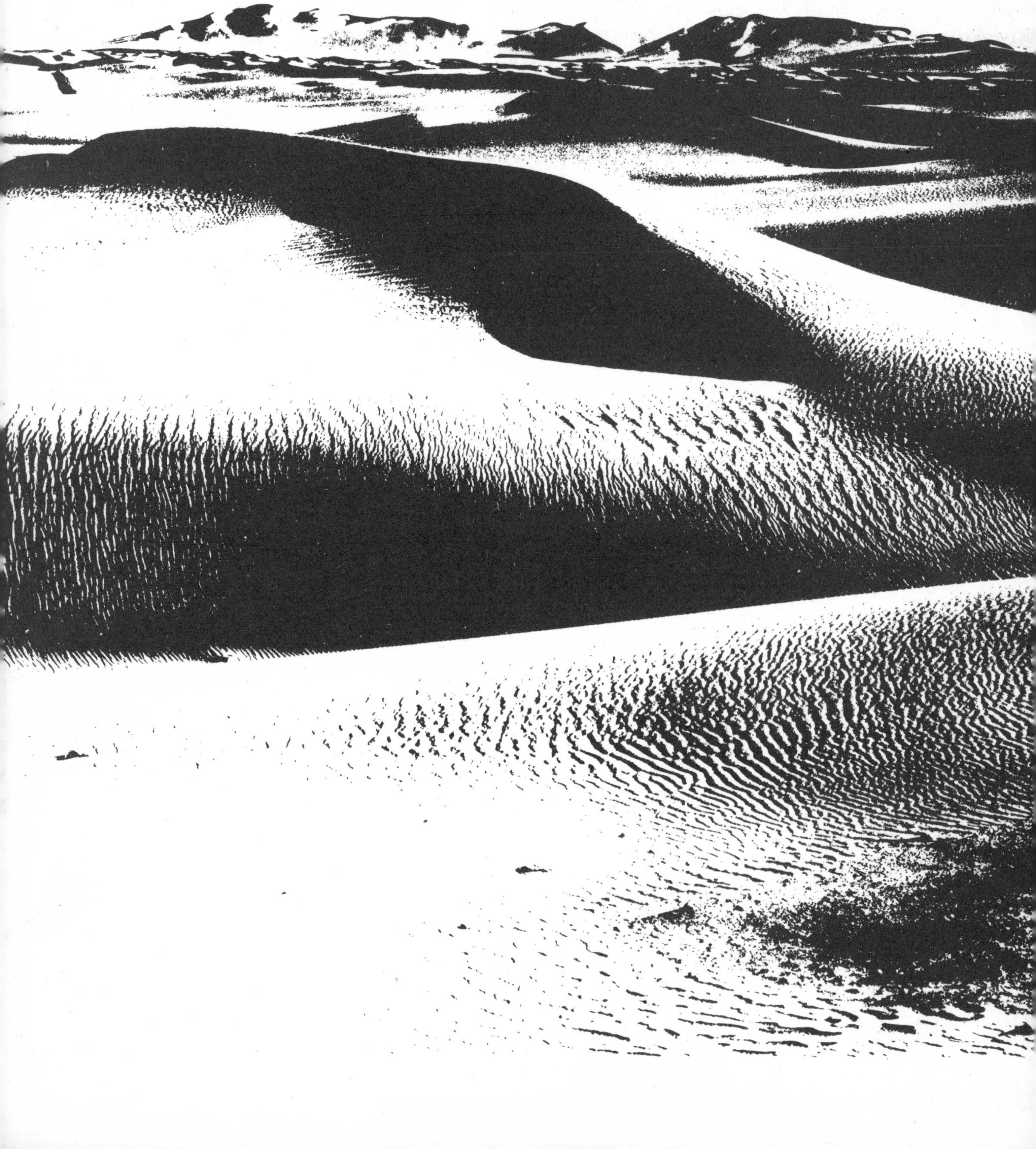